SIMPLY MING

SIMPLY MING

EASY TECHNIQUES FOR
EAST-MEETS-WEST MEALS

Ming Tsai and Arthur Boehm
Photographs by Alan Richardson

CLARKSON POTTER/PUBLISHERS
NEW YORK

To David and Henry, thank you for making every day a perfect day
And Pooh . . . more each day.
M. T.

And for Richard Getke, still the best dining partner.
A. B.

Text copyright © 2003 by Ming Tsai

Photographs copyright © 2003 by Alan Richardson

Published by Clarkson Potter/Publishers, New York, New York
Member of the Crown Publishing Group, a division of Random House, Inc.
www.randomhouse.com

CLARKSON N. POTTER is a trademark and POTTER and colophon are registered trademarks of Random House, Inc.

Printed in Japan

Design by Subtitle-NYC

Library of Congress Cataloging-in-Publication Data is available upon request

ISBN 0-609-61067-8

10 9 8 7 6 5 4 3 2 1

First Edition

ACKNOWLEDGMENTS

To my coauthor, Arthur "Artie" Boehm, who again patiently and masterfully put my passion on paper.

Many thanks to my photographer, Alan Richardson, and his assistant, Roy Galaday, absolutely the best in the business.

To WGBH, coproducer of *Simply Ming*—my gratitude.

To my agent, Michael Carlisle, without whose support this book would not have come to fruition.

Of course, to my parents, Stephen and Iris Tsai, for their love, support, and for putting me on this planet!

And last but not least, to the entire Blue Ginger team, especially Jon, Terrence, Isaac, Rob, Paula, Ben, Marina, Kathleen, K-Man, C.K., Bear, and Suzanne my sincere thanks and appreciation.

M. T.

With thanks, as ever, to Ming Tsai, teacher and friend.

Deep and abiding appreciation also to Judy ("Jinx") Gingold, the Dowager Empress Intestate, and to Alfred Gingold, Helen Rogan, and my ever-lengthening godchild, Toby Rogan Gingold. Thanks also to Laura Karp and Ethan Signer, to John Kane, and, of course, Nick Malgieri, Master of Sweet.

A. B.

Both authors would like to thank their superlative editor and friend, Pam Krauss. Thanks also to her former assistant, Adina Steiman.

Much appreciation also to managing editor Amy Boorstein; production manager Derek McNally; associate art director Jane Treuhaft; copyeditor Janet McDonald; and to the design team at Subtitle NYC.

And, of course, many thanks to executive publicist Barbara Marks, associate publicist Melissa Kay, and to publisher Lauren Shakely.

CONTENTS

RECIPE INDEX

SALADS AND VEGETARIAN ENTREES

Avocado-Stuffed Spicy Crab Salad, 60
Grilled Portobello Sandwich with Roasted
    Pepper-Lemongrass Sambal, 67
Tofu-Mushroom Quesadilla with Tomato-
    Kaffir Lime Salsa, 104
Warm Shiitake and Corn Salad Frisée, 119
Grilled Asian Antipasto Salad, 120
Marinated Tomato Salad with Sesame-
    Crusted Goat Cheese, 125
Warm Rock Shrimp and Celery Root Salad, 126
Grilled Five-Herb Vegetable Panzanella, 128
Wok-Stirred Mushroom Salad Cups, 129
Asian Chicken Salad with Baby Hearts of
    Romaine, 133
Thai Lime Chicken Salad, 143
Sweet Potato Pie with Carrot-
    Chipotle Syrup, 180
Broiled Stuffed Eggplant with Black
    Pepper-Garlic Sauce, 225

NOODLES/RICE/PASTA

Asian Pesto Turkey Spaghetti, 30
My Crazy Chicken-Rice Noodle Stir-Fry, 63
Orzo with Sausage and Roasted Pepper-
    Lemongrass Sambal, 71
Tomato-Kaffir Lime Turkey "Bolognese," 105
Green Curry Chicken Noodles, 109
Seared Tuna with Soba Noodle Salad and
    Soy-Kaffir Lime Dressing, 175
Five-Spice Beef Noodle Soup, 187
Rock Shrimp Miso Risotto with
    Spinach, 202
Tea-Rubbed Shrimp Fried Rice, 232

BURGERS AND SANDWICHES

Asian Sloppy Joes, 53
Grilled Portobello Sandwich with Roasted
    Pepper-Lemongrass Sambal, 67
Asian Lamb "Gyros" with Tomato-Kaffir
    Lime Tzatziki, 101
Salmon Burger with Tomato-Kaffir
    Lime Salsa, 102
Tofu-Mushroom Quesadilla with
    Tomato-Kaffir Lime Salsa, 104
Green Curry Chicken Burger, 112
Pan-Seared Soy-Dijon Hamburger on
    Toast, 157
Panko-Crusted Chicken Sandwich, 224
Asian Hamburger Pockets, 243

APPETIZERS/SIDES/SOUPS

Curry-Ginger Sweet Potato Fries, 25
Spicy Crab Cakes, 59
Pork and Ginger-Fuji Apple Chutney
    Pot Stickers, 75
Potato Pancakes with Apple-Scallion
    Cream, 81
Spicy Cucumber-Kimchee Rice-Noodle
    Soup, 89
Warm Shiitake and Corn Salad Frisée, 119
Grilled Asian Antipasto Salad, 120
Marinated Tomato Salad with Sesame-
    Crusted Goat Cheese, 125
Warm Rock Shrimp and Celery
    Root Salad, 126
Wok-Stirred Mushroom Salad Cups, 129
Scallop and Mango Ceviche, 139
Blue Ginger Crispy Calamari, 140
Grilled Miso-Citrus Scallop Lollipops, 148
Soy-Dijon Chicken Wings, 158
Lemongrass Coconut Chicken Soup, 196
Hot and Sour Shrimp Soup, 199
Miso Soup with Tofu and Nori, 205
Panko-Crusted Soft-Shell Crab with
    Dim Sum Dipper, 222
Blue Ginger Cracker, 239
Scallion Pancakes, 240

DESSERTS

Classic Shortbread, 247
Five-Spice Shortbread, 247
Double Chocolate-Ginger
    Shortbread, 248
Caramel Macadamia Nut Crunch, 249
Tahitian Crème Anglaise, 250
Tahitian Vanilla Ice Cream, 252
Berries Gratiné, 253
Pineapple Custard, 255
Bittersweet Chocolate Ganache, 256
Warm Chocolate Soufflé Cakes with
    Cardamom Cream, 259
Sesame Macadamia Nut, and Dried Fruit
    Chocolate Truffles, 260
Bittersweet Chocolate Pots de
    Crème, 261
Asian Banana Split, 263
Tropical Fruit Salsa, 264
Tropical Fruit Yogurt Parfait, 267
Tropical Fruit Granita, 268
Frozen Tropical Fruit Martinis, 268

INTRODUCTION

When I first began to share my East–West cooking style, I was happy that people understood and embraced this marriage of two culinary traditions. Dishes I served at my Wellesley, Massachusetts restaurant, Blue Ginger, like Beef and Shiitake Stew with Garlic Mashers and Crispy Scallops with Carrot–Star Anise Syrup won over skeptics to the East-Meets-West way, and the ready availability of Asian ingredients made this kind of cooking more accessible than ever to home cooks.

Still, despite the growing interest in East–West cooking, many cooks seem intimidated about tackling it at home. Customers and viewers of my television shows asked me if they could really create something both delicious and wonderful to look at without the kind of crew I have at the restaurant. Many thought that East–West cooking necessarily involved hours of prep time and other kitchen work that was beyond the time-pressed cook on a daily basis. I knew there was a way to make my East-Meets-West approach an every-night proposition, not "event cooking" that's reserved for the weekends and special occasions. At the same time, I wanted to offer up the same great flavor contrasts and tantalizing ingredient pairings that are our Blue Ginger signature. "Fast" would be the goal, but never at the expense of flavor or quality. It's easy to make bad food quickly (and equally easy to take all day and get the same poor results). The challenge was to provide recipes that aren't stripped down versions of the way we cook at Blue Ginger, but are great in themselves.

The breakthrough came when I realized how many of Blue Ginger's signature dishes are based on easily storable flavor bases like Curry-Ginger Oil and Three-Vinegar Syrup—"master" ingredients that become the basis of a wide range of dishes like Wok-Stirred Curry-Ginger Chicken with Zucchini and Seared Halibut with Warm Fennel and Yellow Finn Potato Salad. Preparing these bases in advance and having them at hand when an order comes in means we can transform a handful of fresh ingredients into a great dish in a flash. With the bases on hand, we save precious time (crucial, obviously, in a restaurant setting) and do away with much of the last-minute prep work.

I began sneaking home some of our master ingredients, to use when I cooked for my family. I soon saw that they worked perfectly in everyday, home-cooking situations. With Asian Pesto on hand, for example, I was able to whip up Asian Pesto Turkey Spaghetti in minutes. With Green Curry Paste, it took no time at all to create Grilled Green Curry–Marinated Salmon and Eggplant Steaks. Desserts, too. With Tahitian Crème Anglaise in the fridge I could make terrific Berries Gratiné in almost as little time as it took me to run out for a pint of Häagen-Dazs Swiss Almond; Bittersweet Chocolate Pots de Crème were a breeze once I had a stash of Bittersweet Chocolate Ganache. (Recipes for all these dishes are in the book.)

I soon realized I could write a cookbook based on this storable-master-ingredient approach that would work for *all* cooks. This is it, a book that offers not only great eating, but a foolproof system that helps any cook create East–West food in a snap.

As you'll see, these dishes are the real thing, made super-approachable by the use of a wide and inventive range of master ingredients. And the dishes cover all courses and dining situations, from casual family meals to elegant entertaining.

I also provide the kind of detailed storage information you need (with "use by" dates) to make keeping these flavor bases as foolproof as using them.

I hope you'll enjoy as well as rely on the *Simply Ming* approach—and devise your own master ingredients and uses. I always like cookbooks that teach.

As a chef, my job is to make people happy with my food. Most cooks, I think, share this impulse, which is, unfortunately, sometimes challenged by tight schedules or by day-end fatigue. With *Simply Ming,* you can make those you feed very, very happy without taxing your own ability to get real food on the table fast.

And always, peace and good eating.

TIPS FOR USING THIS BOOK

- Start by perusing the book. Look for dishes that call out to you, then work backward to find the master ingredient from which each is made. Then figure out when you can easily make the base. Most people will find the weekend best for this, though many of the bases are simple enough to put together in the morning for that evening. Once you have the base on hand, or stored away, consider when within its allotted storage time you'll put it to use; that way you can plan your shopping for multiple meals and reduce the need for last-minute dashes to the market.

- For most of the flavor-based recipes, one batch will be enough to make all the dishes each is designed for. This prevents you from having to redouble cooking effort, a *Simply Ming* theme. But you can halve the master recipes, if you like. Generally, though, I advise you make more so you can enjoy more.

- Keep storage in mind. Bases like Master Meat Broth require space in the freezer or fridge. Make sure you have cleared enough space, and be sure to label every container with the date the base was made, especially important for anything that goes into the freezer.

- As noted in the recipes, some ingredients like Asian Pesto will darken over time. Though it might not be as pretty as it was when you made it, it will taste even better as the flavors have a chance to blend and intensify. Do not, however, exceed the recommended storage time for any flavor base. This shouldn't be a problem, as I see it, since you'll want to make these dishes right away once you see how quick and easy they truly are.

- The best all-around receptacles in which to store most things are screw-top glass jars—large empty mayonnaise or mustard jars work beautifully. Make sure the jars are clean before adding the ingredients.

- Some ingredients can be frozen very successfully, others are best refrigerated. Check recipes for storage recommendations, including "use-by" times.

- Never put a finger in the master ingredients, which can introduce unwanted bacteria. Always use spoons or chopsticks for tasting.

SIMPLE INGREDIENTS
SEASONINGS, CONDIMENTS, AND AROMATICS

Fish Sauce. Made from salted and fermented anchovies, fish sauce is a staple South Asian flavoring. I prefer the Thai version, which is called nam pla. Look for the Three Crab brand, which has a fresh sea taste and slight sweetness.

Five-Spice Powder. This delightfully fragrant Chinese seasoning consists usually of ground star anise, Szechwan peppercorns, clove, fennel, and cinnamon. The powder should be aromatic and bright in color, and keep it that way by storing it tightly enclosed in a cool, dry place.

I created **eight-spice powder** by adding ginger, allspice, cardamom, and cumin to the basic five-spice mix and omitting the Szechwan peppercorns so it works beautifully as a flavoring for sweet as well as savory dishes. You can order eight-spice powder from ming.com.

Kecap Manis. This traditional Indonesian soy sauce has a sweeter, more complex flavor than its Chinese and Japanese equivalents. It's also thicker. Look for the ABC brand from Indonesia.

Mirin. An essential Japanese ingredient that adds mild sweetness to a range of dishes, glazes, and sauces, mirin is a rice wine with sugar added. I recommend hon-mirin, which is naturally brewed and contains natural sugars, rather than aji-mirin, which can contain other sweeteners.

Miso. Miso is a thick, soybean-based flavoring paste. Of the four main types, which range in saltiness and depth of flavor, milder white miso (shiro-miso), made with rice, is the kind I call for in this book. Stored in the fridge it will last for three months.

Hoisin Sauce. This traditional Chinese ingredient is made from soybean paste, sugar, garlic, and vinegar, has a slightly sweet, spicy flavor. I always like to cook hoisin sauce in oil for a few minutes before adding it to dishes to rid it of its raw bean flavor. A brand I like is Koon Chuung.

Ponzu. This Japanese dressing adds sprightly citrus tang to sashimi and other dishes. Traditionally made with citronlike yuzu peel, and juice from sudachi, a small green Japanese citrus fruit, it's also available flavored with lemon or lime juice. Avoid ponzu made with soy sauce, a type widely available that's best for dipping. Marukan ponzu is available at most supermarkets.

Soy Sauce. Soy sauces vary in richness, saltiness, and flavor depending on where and how they're produced. Dark soy sauce, which is aged longer than the lighter kind and usually made with molasses, is thicker and more intensely flavored, though never as salty as the regular kind. Among the regular sauces, I like Japanese Kikkoman Soy Sauce and the Chinese brands Koon Chun's Thin Soy Sauce and Pearl River Bridge Superior Soy Sauce. My favorite dark soy sauces—sometimes labeled "black soy sauce" or "soy superior sauce"—are Koon Chun Black Soy Sauce and Amoy's. Never buy soy sauces produced from hydrolyzed vegetable protein; look for "naturally brewed" on labels.

Tea Leaves. In this book I call for two tea types to be used as rub ingredients: lapsang souchong, China's venerable black tea, which is noted for is deep smokiness, and mint green tea, nonfermented tea leaves that are flavored with mint.

Thai Bird Chiles. These fiery, bullet-shaped-peppers, also called bird's eye chiles and bird peppers, are available fresh and dried at Asian markets. Their name derives from the belief that they were first harvested by birds said to enjoy eating them. If unavailable, I recommend that you substitute equal quantities per weight of dried serrano chiles.

Lemongrass. Used traditionally in Southeast Asian cooking, this aromatic citrusy ingredient resembles large, stiff-leafed scallions. Use only the portion of the stalks from the base to the point where the leaves branch out.

Thai Basil. This wonderfully fragrant herb called *bai horapa* in Asian markets has small green leaves and purple stems. Its flavor is reminiscent of anise mixed with more familiar sweet-basil flavors. Store the basil refrigerated with its root ends in water, covered with a plastic bag.

Fermented Black Beans. A mainstay of Southern Chinese cooking, this pungent ingredient is made from small black soybeans that are flavored with salt and spices and then allowed to ferment. Store the beans, which are usually sold in bags, away from light in a cool, dry place. The beans will last indefinitely.

Kaffir Lime Leaves. This Thai seasoning, taken from kaffir lime trees, has a delightfully pungent, limelike fragrance. Most desirable fresh, the leaves are also available frozen or dried. If the leaf itself is to be eaten, remove the center rib.

OILS AND VINEGARS

Rice Wine Vinegar. Lightly acidic, this white to amber vinegar is, as its name suggests, made from fermented rice. For the recipes in this book, avoid seasoned versions.

Grapeseed Oil. This is my preferred vegetable cooking oil because it's very low in saturated fats and has a high smoke point, which makes it excellent for sautéing and wok-cooking. (It also makes fine vinaigrettes.) Expressed, as you might think, from grape seed, the oil also has a pleasing, slightly nutty flavor. **Canola Oil** is the next best choice. It has a clean "natural" flavor and only 6 percent saturated fat.

Asian Sesame Oil. Not to be confused with almost-flavorless refined sesame oils, this thick, dark oil has a distinctly nutty taste and aroma. Because of its rich flavor, it's used as a seasoning rather than for cooking.

Chinese Black Vinegar. Made usually from glutinous rice, this very dark vinegar is appealingly deep-flavored. Quality varies; the better brands have a complex richness reminiscent of balsamic vinegars. A brand I like is Chin Kiang.

NOODLES AND RICE

Shanghai Noodles. This thick, oval wheat noodle—most types are $1/4$ inch wide—is a regional favorite. The noodles are usually packaged in 1-pound bags.

Rice Noodles. Sometimes called rice stick noodles, these mildly flavored rice-flour noodles are never cooked, but instead soaked in warm water until softened. They're available in a range of sizes; I recommend those that are $1/4$ inch thick.

Soba Noodles. These Japanese noodles are made with buckwheat flour, which gives them their distinctively earthy flavor. They are traditionally served cold with a dashi-soy dipping sauce or in broths.

Sushi Rice. Moderately sticky when cooked, this short-grain rice is domestically grown and marketed under brand names, including Kumai Harvest and Koshi Hikari. Its texture when cooked makes it ideal for preparing rolled and hand-shaped sushi; it also makes great risotto.

OTHER INGREDIENTS

Coconut Milk. Made from a simmering mixture of dried coconut and water, this flavorful ingredient should not be confused with cream of coconut, which is sweetened. Since coconut milk separates on standing, always shake the can well before using.

Shrimp. Shrimp are almost always shipped to market frozen and defrosted for sale. So don't hesitate to buy frozen shrimp and defrost them at home. Contessa's peeled and deveined shrimp are great time savers. **Rock Shrimp** have a delicious lobsterlike flavor and come already peeled because their shells resist removal. If you can't find them, substitute regular shrimp cut into $1/2$-inch pieces.

Sambal Oelek. A popular Southeast Asian condiment, sambal oelek is, at its simplest, a fiery mixture of chiles, brown sugar, and salt. Sambal oelek, and other sambal types, have many variations, though, and can include ingredients like kaffir lime leaves, tamarind, and coconut milk. When buying sambal oelek, look for those imported from Asia or the domestic Hung Fong Foods brand.

SIMPLE TECHNIQUES

Stir-Frying. The key to successful stir-frying is a properly preheated wok. This can be difficult to achieve on conventional Western stoves, which usually lack enough burner heat. Instead, preheat your wok in the oven. To do this, use metal-handled woks only. Preheat your oven to 450°F. and heat a dry wok until the wok is very hot, about 5 minutes. Making sure that your hands are *very* well protected with heavy kitchen gloves, remove the wok by its handles and place it on the stove top, over the highest heat. Add oil as you normally do and proceed, making sure you don't overcrowd the wok, or your ingredients will steam rather than sear.

Slicing Beef Thinly. If you don't have a home deli-type slicer, the easiest way to get thinly sliced meat is to put it in the freezer until the meat is slightly hard, about 30 to 45 minutes, depending on meat thickness. Remove and slice using a cleaver or very sharp, thin-bladed knife.

Blanching Pasta. This flavor- and texture-saving method is great for pasta, allowing it to be precooked and held for finishing later. Be sure to have a large bowl or sink filled with ice water. Cook the pasta until almost al dente, a few minutes less than box instructions advise. Long pasta like spaghetti should retain a pinhole of rawness at the center. Drain the pasta, shock it in the cold-water bath, and drain again. You can hold the pasta in the colander; it shouldn't stick to itself, but if it seems as if it might, toss it lightly with a little oil.

Correcting with Salt and Pepper. You'll notice that I often advice you to correct dish seasoning with salt and pepper. This instruction, which I sometimes give more than once in a recipe, reflects the fact that salt and pepper added at one point can change in strength or flavor depending on subsequent cooking and cooling. Make sure to taste a dish frequently throughout its preparation, making the necessary seasoning adjustments as you go along. Get into the habit of tasting and "correcting" and your cooking will soar.

Preheating Pans for Searing. You can give yourself a leg up when searing meats and vegetables by preheating the pan in which they'll sear in a 400°F. and 500°F. oven for about 5 minutes. Make sure the pan has ovenproof handles. You'll be delighted in the difference it makes in the quality of the sear you get—and the time you save.

Using Stockpots for Frying. Here's a technique that makes so much sense, I wonder why more cooks aren't wise to it. If you lack an electric deep-fryer, the easiest and most messless receptacle for deep-frying is a stockpot. Its relatively tall sides ensure less kitchen splatter while its comparatively narrow dimension means you'll need less oil to get the job done. Incidentally, the best tool for retrieving deep-fried food is a Chinese strainer, which has a wide, open-mesh skimmer and long bamboo handle.

Roll Cutting. This traditional Chinese slicing method, which maximizes surface area for quick cooking and flavoring penetration, is usually applied to cylindrical vegetables like carrots, asparagus, and certain squash. To roll-cut these, first make a diagonal slice near the stem end of one vegetable piece and discard the end. You want to cut at an angle that's neither too acute nor too wide. Now roll the object one-quarter to one-third turn away from you and slice again at the same angle about 1 inch farther along the vegetable. Continue rolling and cutting until the ingredient has been reduced to segments with diagonally cut—though not parallel—ends. (When cutting asparagus, the "final" segment should be sliced on one end only and thus include the tip.)

FLAVORED OILS
AND SAUCES

Flavored oils are everywhere today, used mostly to make vinaigrettes or as a bread dip. But there is more to the flavored-oil story. The Curry-Ginger Oil in this chapter gives your cooking a terrific boost. As a frying medium, its subtle curry flavor lends great taste to dishes like Wok-Stirred Curry-Ginger Beef and Leeks, Wok-Stirred Curry-Ginger Chicken and Zucchini and terrific Curry-Ginger Sweet Potato Fries.

The sauces in this chapter work similarly. With easily made Asian Pesto on hand, for example, you add tantalizing ginger, cilantro, and garlic flavor plus chile heat to shrimp and radicchio as they're grilled, and for another taste layer before they're served. Black Bean–Garlic Sauce, based on the traditional Chinese marriage of black beans and garlic, is equally versatile and has so much *oomph,* you'll use it all the time. (Try adding it to noodles.) Begin, though, with Wok-Stirred Beef with Eggplant and Black Beans and Black Bean Pork and Tofu Stir-Fry, which use the sauce to enhance the subtle flavors of eggplant and tofu as well as meat.

Black Pepper–Garlic Sauce is another East-West meld that adds flavor depth to dishes like Blue Ginger Black Pepper–Garlic Lobster, a signature specialty from the restaurant you can make at home easily.

Hoisin-Lime Sauce was inspired by my grandmother, who used hoisin sauce as a condiment, even putting it on pizza! I use Hoisin-Lime Sauce to make the best Sloppy Joes ever, as well as a Hoisin-Roasted Duck with Sweet Potatoes, where it works like a barbecue sauce. In fact, I think of it as Asian barbecue sauce, and recommend you use it as you would more traditional grilling sauces.

MASTER RECIPE

TRY IT

Toss veggies like zucchini, onions, or peppers with the oil, season them with salt and pepper, and bake them on a baking sheet that's been preheated in a 400°F. oven. You can also grill them outdoors.

Use the oil to make a deliciously spicy vinaigrette.

For a quick supper dish, sauté sea scallops in the oil.

MING'S TIP

Curry powders can be a marvelous flavoring, depending on the brand and its freshness. My preferred blend is called, and sometimes labeled, Madras Curry Powder. It's usually a well-balanced mixture of curry leaves, turmeric, coriander, cumin, cinnamon, cloves, chiles, bay leaves, fenugreek, allspice, and black pepper. Shop for it in Indian markets, where turnover is rapid.

CURRY-GINGER OIL

People often tell me they love the taste of curry, but not the kick many curried dishes deliver. For anyone who wants subtly fragrant curried taste in their cooking, this oil is a must. Just try Curry-Ginger Sweet Potato Fries and you'll see exactly what I mean.

I recommend Madras curry powder. It has a deeper, "darker" flavor than other curry powders, due to its relative abundance of cinnamon, allspice, and clove. After steeping with the oil, the spices will settle to the bottom of your jar. You'll want to scoop out and use the bright yellow oil (an old spoon bent at a 45-degree angle makes a perfect dipper) and leave the spice behind.

If you're not using the oil for frying, you can make a half or even quarter batch of oil if you prefer.

Makes 1 quart
Lasts 1 month, refrigerated

1 quart grapeseed or canola oil
$1/2$ cup peeled and minced fresh ginger
1 cup Madras curry powder

1. In a large, heavy saucepan, combine the oil with the ginger and heat over medium heat until the oil is fragrant and the ginger just begins to color, about 8 minutes. Remove from the heat and cool completely, about 20 minutes.

2. Meanwhile, place a large, heavy sauté pan over medium heat. Add the curry powder to the dry skillet and toast, stirring, until the curry powder smokes slightly, 8 to 10 minutes. Whisk in the ginger and oil, remove from the stove, and cool completely, 30 to 40 minutes.

3. Transfer the oil and spices to a 1- to $1/2$-quart glass jar, scraping the pan well. Allow the mixture to stand until the oil and curry powder have separated completely, about 4 hours or overnight. The oil is now ready to use. Store in the refrigerator.

BEVERAGE TIP
Grape type
Sauvignon Blanc

Characteristics
Citrusy, grass and herb
notes, some wet stone

Recommendations
Lucien Crochet
"Le Chene"
Loire, France

Cain Musque
Monterey, California

WOK-STIRRED CURRY-GINGER CHICKEN WITH ZUCCHINI

Curried chicken is probably the most ubiquitous curry dish in America—not necessarily high praise. But this quickly cooked version, featuring crispy zucchini, really shines. Stir-frying not only ensures fresh flavor, it also means healthier food, as little oil is needed for cooking. And the dish, with its vivid golden color, looks beautiful.

If you're concerned about fat in your diet, you can substitute chicken breasts for the thighs, though the thighs have richer flavor and are used here without their skin.

Serve this family style, on a platter of rice.

Serves 4

1 1/2 pounds boneless, skinless chicken thighs cut into 1/2-inch dice
1 tablespoon cornstarch
4 tablespoons Curry-Ginger Oil (page 18)
Kosher salt and freshly ground black pepper to taste
2 medium yellow or white onions, cut into 1-inch dice
2 small zucchini, roll-cut into 1-inch lengths (see page 15)
1/2 cup Master Chicken Broth (page 192) or low-sodium canned chicken broth
   or vegetable stock

1. In a medium bowl, combine the chicken and cornstarch and mix to coat the chicken completely.

2. Heat a wok or large, heavy sauté pan over high heat. Add 2 tablespoons of the Curry-Ginger Oil and swirl to coat the pan. Add the chicken and stir-fry until just cooked through, 3 to 5 minutes. Season with salt and pepper. Remove the chicken to a plate.

3. Reheat the wok over high heat. Add 1 tablespoon of the oil and swirl to coat the pan. Add the onions and stir-fry until the onions are soft, about 2 minutes. Add the zucchini, season with salt and pepper, and stir-fry until the zucchini is tender, 4 to 5 minutes. Return the chicken to the wok, add the broth, and bring it to a boil, about 30 seconds. Stir, remove from the stove, and correct the seasoning. Drizzle with the remaining tablespoon of oil and serve immediately.

BEVERAGE TIP

Grape type

Gamay

Characteristics

Clean, lightly roasted
red berry, spice nuance

Recommendations

Chateau de Pizay
Beaujolais, France

Desvignes
Beaujolais, France

Serve slightly chilled

MING'S TIP

To clean the leeks easily,
slice them directly into a
bowl of water, swish them
around to remove any grit,
let the grit settle to the
bottom, then lift the leeks
out with a strainer and dry
them in a salad spinner.

WOK-STIRRED CURRY-GINGER BEEF AND LEEKS

Beef and onions is a classic Asian combo. Here, the marriage achieves a higher plane by using the royal onion—leeks. Leeks are similar in flavor to scallions, often used in Asian cooking, but they're much more versatile (try them in marinades) and much sweeter when cooked. They're great in this savory curry and ginger–flavored stir-fry.

Serves 4

2 tablespoons Curry-Ginger Oil (page 18)
1 pound flank steak, cut across the grain into 1-inch slices
Kosher salt and freshly ground black pepper to taste
3 large leeks, white and light green parts only, cut into $1/4$-inch rings,
   washed and well dried
1 medium red bell pepper, cored and cut into $1/2$-inch dice

1. Heat a wok or large, heavy sauté pan over high heat. Add the Curry-Ginger Oil and swirl to coat the pan. Add the beef and stir-fry until it's medium-rare, about 2 minutes. Season with salt and pepper.

2. Add the leeks to the wok and stir-fry until softened, about 2 minutes. Add the bell pepper and stir-fry for 1 minute. Season with salt and pepper. Toss one more time, remove from the stove, and serve immediately.

CURRY-GINGER SWEET POTATO FRIES

I "discovered" these terrific curry-flavored fries when I cooked at Silks in San Francisco. Unlike the thinner version we made there, these "steak fries" are prepared with unpeeled sweet potatoes, which are easier to cut into fries than other potatoes. These bigger fries not only give you more to love, they are healthier, due to the unpeeled sweets and the fact they're baked, not fried.

These are perfect with burgers and steaks, of course, but try them also with roast chicken—an amazing match.

Serves 4

4 large sweet potatoes, scrubbed and unpeeled
1 cup Curry-Ginger Oil (page 18), plus 2 tablespoons for drizzling
1 bunch of scallions, green and white parts, thinly sliced
Kosher salt and freshly ground black pepper to taste

1. Trim 1/4 inch from the ends of each potato, then shave the sides to make rough rectangular shapes. Cut the potatoes lengthwise into 1/2-inch-wide slices. Stack the slices and cut into 1/2-inch-wide fries. Dry the potatoes well.

2. In a large bowl, combine the 1 cup of Curry-Ginger Oil and all but 2 tablespoons of the scallions. Add the potatoes, season with salt and pepper, and toss well.

3. Place a heavy sheet pan or large, heavy skillet in the oven and heat to 400°F. Remove the pan, dump the fries onto it, and, using a spatula, separate the potatoes. (The potatoes should sizzle when they touch the pan; if they don't, remove them from the pan, return it to the oven, and continue to heat it. Then return the potatoes to the pan.)

4. Bake the potatoes until golden brown, 10 to 15 minutes. Check periodically to make sure the potatoes aren't browning too quickly.

5. With a spatula, turn the potatoes and continue to cook until the uncolored side is golden, 10 to 15 minutes more. If the bottoms are browning too rapidly, turn the potatoes and lower the heat to 350°F. Check for doneness with a toothpick; it should penetrate the potatoes easily.

6. Arrange the potatoes on a serving platter, toss with the remaining scallions and oil, correct the seasoning, and serve hot.

BEVERAGE TIP

Beer
Characteristics
Five Spice and
orange zest, yeasty

Recommendations
Belgian style:
Chimay Blanc
Belgium

Ommegang, Hennepin
Cooperstown, New York

MING'S TIP

For the crispest fries,
rinse the cut potatoes
in hot water 3 times,
drain, and soak in a
bowl of hot water for
30 minutes, then drain
and dry them well. This
removes excess starch
to help ensure crisping.

MASTER RECIPE

TRY IT

For a great chip dip, mix equal parts of the pesto with softened cream cheese.

Use the pesto as a sandwich spread; it's particularly good with chicken salad or grilled portobello mushroom fillings.

Mix 1 part pesto with 2 parts chopped shrimp. Use as a filling for dumplings made with store-bought wonton skins. Deep-fry the dumplings until golden and serve as an hors d'oeuvre.

ASIAN PESTO

I'll admit it: The Chinese didn't invent pesto. The giveaways are the cheese and pine nuts, two indisputably Western ingredients that help make it delicious—and rich. My East—West version, which adds ginger, cilantro, and chile heat to the basic basil-garlic mix, is much lighter than the Italian original. It makes a temptingly spicy flavoring for pasta and much more.

The pesto stays vibrant in color and flavor for at least a week; after that, it will darken but will still taste great for another week. Stir the sauce well before using it.

Makes about $3^1/_2$ cups
Lasts 2 weeks, refrigerated

2 jalapeño chiles, stemmed and seeded
8 garlic cloves
1 tablespoon sugar
1 heaping tablespoon peeled and minced fresh ginger
1 cup roasted salted macadamia nuts or roasted salted peanuts
Zest of 2 lemons
2 cups extra-virgin olive oil
1 cup fresh basil leaves, packed
1 cup fresh mint leaves, packed
$1/_2$ cup fresh cilantro leaves, packed
Kosher salt and freshly ground black pepper to taste

In a blender or food processor, combine the chiles, garlic, sugar, ginger, nuts, zest, and 1 cup of the oil and blend until smooth. Add the basil, mint, and cilantro and blend while slowly adding the remaining oil until a thick purée is formed. Season with salt and pepper. Store in a tightly covered jar and refrigerate.

ASIAN PESTO CHICKEN SALAD

If ubiquity means anything, pasta salad with chicken ranks right up there in popularity with hamburgers and cole slaw on the American picnic table. But too often it can be bland or heavy. This spicy grilled-chicken version gives you all the satisfaction of everyday pasta salads and more. First, instead of the usual fusilli, it's made with orzo, whose small rice shapes coat beautifully. Second, the salad's dairy free, so you can serve it at room temperature without worry. Finally, it goes together really quickly—good news when you want a delicious but unstressful party dish.

Make this with warm or room-temperature chicken, as you prefer—and, for best texture, avoid tossing the ingredients together until the last minute.

Serves 4

2 tablespoons grapeseed or canola oil, if needed
1½ cups uncooked orzo
4 boneless chicken breasts with skin
Kosher salt and freshly ground black pepper to taste
1¼ cups Asian Pesto (page 26), plus additional for drizzling
1 pint cherry tomatoes, halved
Juice of 2 lemons
½ pound baby spinach, washed and dried

1. Prepare an outdoor grill, heat to hot, and spray the grid with nonstick cooking oil. Alternatively, heat a grill pan or heavy sauté pan over high heat, add the oil, and swirl to coat the pan.

2. Bring a large saucepan of lightly salted water to a boil. Cook the orzo until just tender, about 10 minutes. Drain well.

3. Meanwhile, season the chicken on both sides with salt and pepper. Grill the chicken, turning once, until the juices run clear when the meat is pierced with the tip of a paring knife, about 10 minutes. Alternatively, grill the breasts in a pan over medium-high heat, turning once, until cooked through, about 10 minutes. Cut the chicken with its skin into ¼-inch-wide slices. Allow the chicken to come to room temperature if you prefer, or proceed with the warm chicken slices.

4. In a large bowl, combine the chicken with 1 cup of the pesto, the orzo, and the tomatoes. Season with salt and pepper. In a medium bowl, combine the remaining ¼ cup of pesto with the lemon juice, then toss with the spinach. Season with salt and pepper.

5. Divide the spinach mixture among 4 plates. Mound the chicken salad on the spinach, drizzle with additional pesto, and serve.

BEVERAGE TIP

Grape type
Pinot Grigio

Characteristics
Crisp, juicy, fresh, bone-dry

Recommendations
Livio Felluga
Friuli, Italy

Santa Margherita
Alto Adige, Italy

MING'S TIPS

When using a grill pan or skillet, I add about ¼ cup of water to the pan as the breasts approach doneness. The resulting steam completes the cooking quickly and adds moisture.

If you have leftovers, combine them with chicken broth for a totally tasty, totally easy soup (add 2 cups of broth for every cup of salad). Drizzle some Asian Pesto on each portion, and don't confess when your guests applaud your great dish.

BEVERAGE TIP

Grape type
Riesling,
Gewürztraminer,
Pinot Blanc, Pinot Gris,
Sylvaner, Müller
Thurgau, Sémillon,
Chardonnay, Muscat

Characteristics
Complex, lively mouth
feel, food friendly,
well-balanced

Recommendations
Sokol Blosser Evolution,
American Cuvée

ASIAN PESTO TURKEY SPAGHETTI

This is my takeoff on spaghetti with bolognese sauce. That Italian meat ragù is delicious, but time-consuming to make. Here, lighter turkey stands in for the traditional ground pork and Asian Pesto gives the dish real zing.

I like to finish the spaghetti with a dusting of Parmigiano-Reggiano—it pulls everything together—but feel free to omit it. The dish will still be fabulous.

Serves 4

Kosher salt
1 pound spaghetti, cooked in salted water until al dente, then refreshed in
   ice water (see page 15)
2 tablespoons extra-virgin olive oil
1 large red onion, minced
1 pound ground turkey
1 pound button mushrooms, cut into $1/4$-inch slices
1 cup dry white wine
$1^{1}/_{2}$ cups Asian Pesto (page 26)
Freshly ground black pepper to taste
Grated Parmigiano-Reggiano, for serving (optional)

1. Bring a large pot of salted water to a boil. Add the spaghetti and cook according to package instructions until al dente. Drain well.

2. While the pasta cooks, coat a large, heavy saucepan with the oil and heat over high heat until hot. Add the onion and sauté, stirring, until lightly browned, about 3 minutes. Add the turkey and mushrooms and sauté, breaking up the turkey with a wooden spoon, until the turkey is just cooked through, about 5 minutes. Add the wine and deglaze, scraping the pan to incorporate any brown bits, and cook until the liquid is reduced by half, about 3 minutes.

3. Add the pesto and pasta to the saucepan, toss to coat, and season with salt and pepper. Warm over medium heat to heat the pasta thoroughly and transfer to pasta bowls. Sprinkle with the cheese, if using, and serve.

BEVERAGE TIP
Grape type
Riesling,
Gewürztraminer,
Pinot Blanc, Pinot Gris,
Sylvaner, Müller
Thurgau, Sémillon,
Chardonnay, Muscat

Characteristics
Complex, lively mouth
feel, food friendly,
well-balanced

Recommendations
Sokol Blosser Evolution,
American Cuvée

GRILLED ASIAN PESTO SHRIMP AND RADICCHIO

This easy dish pairs grilled radicchio with shrimp that's been marinated in Asian Pesto and also grilled. The slight bitterness of the radicchio is a wonderful foil for the rich, spicy shrimp and makes the dish a light but savory treat. I particularly enjoy it in summer. It's a great example of how simple ingredients can be transformed when the seasoning's right—and it's a great incentive for having Asian Pesto on hand.

Grill the radicchio and shrimp outdoors, or use a grill pan or heavy skillet.

A photograph of this dish appears on page 6.

Serves 4

1 tablespoon grapeseed or canola oil, for coating the pan, if using
12 extra-large (10- to 15-count) shrimp, peeled (but tails left on), deveined, and butterflied
Kosher salt and freshly ground black pepper to taste
1/2 cup Asian Pesto (page 26), plus additional for garnish
1/4 cup balsamic vinegar
1/4 cup extra-virgin olive oil
2 medium heads of radicchio, halved

1. Prepare an outdoor grill, heat to hot, and spray the grid with nonstick cooking oil. Alternatively, heat a grill pan or heavy sauté pan over high heat. If using a sauté pan, add 1 tablespoon oil and swirl to coat the pan.

2. Meanwhile, season the shrimp lightly with salt and pepper, rub with the pesto, and marinate in the refrigerator for 15 minutes.

3. Grill the shrimp on both sides until just cooked through, 2 minutes per side. Set aside, keeping the shrimp warm.

4. Meanwhile, combine the vinegar with the olive oil in a small bowl. Brush the radicchio on all sides with the mixture and season with salt and pepper. Place the radicchio cut side down on the grill and grill until charred, about 3 minutes. Turn and repeat, about 3 minutes more.

5. Halve the radicchio, core, and arrange 2 wedges on each serving plate. Surround with the shrimp, garnish the plate with the additional Asian Pesto, and serve.

TRY IT

For an easy pasta dish, toss with freshly cooked spaghetti or linguine and raw baby spinach.

The sauce adds terrific flavor to stir-fries. Just toss it with veggies you've stir-fried in oil until tender-crisp and season with salt and pepper to taste.

For an East–West chicken salad, mix the sauce with cooked cubed chicken and pile the mixture onto whole lettuce leaves.

BLACK BEAN–GARLIC SAUCE

As a teenager in Dayton, Ohio, I had to seek out Chinatowns away from home to have black beans and clams, a dish I'd dream about—literally. The combo is classic Chinese, like its main savory seasoning, the black beans and garlic. This version gives you all the great pungent taste of that immortal pairing without the bother of having to chop and blend every time you want it. At Blue Ginger we use this sauce all the time to make the delicious Wok-Stirred Clams and Black Beans on page 35—and you will too, once you have it on hand.

Be sure not to seal the jar in which you store the sauce until it's completely cool, and stir it well before using.

Makes about 3 cups
Lasts 2 weeks, refrigerated

1 cup grapeseed oil or canola oil
$1/3$ cup fermented black beans, roughly chopped
$1/2$ cup minced garlic
$1/2$ cup peeled and minced fresh ginger
2 bunches of scallions, white and green parts, sliced $1/8$ inch thick
1 tablespoon sambal oelek or hot red pepper sauce
$1/2$ cup Shaoxing rice wine or dry sherry
2 teaspoons kosher salt
1 teaspoon freshly ground black pepper

1. Heat a wok or large sauté pan over high heat. Add $1/4$ cup of the oil and swirl to coat the pan. Add the beans, garlic, ginger, and scallions, and stir-fry until the mixture has softened, 2 to 3 minutes.

2. Add the sambal oelek and wine, decrease the heat to medium, and cook until the mixture is reduced by three quarters, 2 to 3 minutes. Add the salt and pepper.

3. Remove the mixture from the heat and allow it to cool. Transfer half of the mixture to a blender and purée it at high speed while adding the remaining $3/4$ cup of oil. Stir the purée back into the remaining mixture and cool completely. Use or store.

WOK-STIRRED CLAMS AND BLACK BEANS

As a Midwesterner, I didn't have clams available locally. Once I tasted them with black beans on the East Coast, though, I was seriously hooked. This easy version of that pairing forgoes the usual cornstarch, so it has a more delicate texture. The addition of basil and tomatoes gives it a very welcome Western flavor, too.

If you're not a clam fancier, you can substitute mussels. Just follow the recipe as written.

Serves 4

2 tablespoons grapeseed or canola oil
2 pounds Manila or littleneck clams, scrubbed
$1/2$ cup Black Bean-Garlic Sauce (page 32)
1 cup Master Chicken Broth (page 192) or homemade or store-bought vegetable stock
1 cup tomatoes cut into $1/4$-inch dice
2 tablespoons fresh basil leaves cut into $1/16$-inch ribbons
1 to 2 tablespoons unsalted butter, as needed
Kosher salt and freshly ground black pepper to taste

Heat a wok or large sauté pan over high heat. Add the oil and swirl to coat the pan. Add the clams and stir-fry until they have opened slightly, 2 to 3 minutes. Add the Black Bean–Garlic Sauce and chicken broth and cook until the liquid is reduced by half, about 2 minutes. Stir in the tomatoes, basil, and butter. Correct the seasoning with salt and pepper and serve immediately.

BEVERAGE TIP

Grape type

Zinfandel blend
(Zinfandel, Petite
Sirah, Carignan)

Characteristics
Jammy, big upfront
berry flavor, explosive

Recommendations
Ridge Lytton Springs
Sonoma County,
California

Ravenswood Zinfandel
Sonoma County,
California

WOK-STIRRED BEEF WITH EGGPLANT AND BLACK BEANS

The full-flavored pungency of black beans complements meats like beef and less delicate seafood. But it also works beautifully with eggplant, which has a slight sweetness that enhances the beans. This delicious dish uses both eggplant and beef for a black bean double-header. It's simple to make and couldn't be more tempting.

Use long Japanese eggplants, if you can. (They're an all-year staple at Asian markets.) Besides being easier to cut, they hold their shape better after cooking than regular eggplants do, and are sweeter.

Serves 4

4 medium Japanese eggplants or 2 medium regular eggplants, cut into $1/2$-dice
Kosher salt and freshly ground black pepper to taste
2 tablespoons grapeseed or canola oil
$1/2$ cup Black Bean–Garlic Sauce (page 32)
1 pound flank steak, cut diagonally into $1/4$-inch slices

1. Place the eggplant on a baking sheet and season with salt and pepper. Set aside for 5 minutes.

2. Heat a wok or large sauté pan over high heat. Add 1 tablespoon of the oil and swirl to coat the pan. Add the eggplant and stir-fry until the eggplant is cooked through, 3 to 5 minutes. Using a slotted spoon, transfer the eggplant to paper towels and drain.

3. Return the wok to high heat, add the remaining tablespoon of oil, and swirl to coat the pan. Add the Black Bean–Garlic Sauce and the beef and stir-fry until the meat is cooked through, about 1 minute. Return the eggplant to the wok and heat through, mixing thoroughly. Correct the seasoning with salt and pepper and serve immediately.

BEVERAGE TIP

Grape type
Tempranillo

Characteristics
Earthy, vanillin,
ripe berry

Recommendations
Rioja Allende
Rioja Alta, Spain

Montecillo Reserva
Rioja, Spain

MING'S TIP
Flip the tofu in this
very gently as it's soft
and inclined to break.
You can practice flip-
ping with rice.

BLACK BEAN PORK AND TOFU STIR-FRY

This is my black-bean version of a traditional Chinese dish, ma po tofu—pork and tofu. The dish may seem baffling to people who think of tofu as a meat stand-in, but it is a classic. Note, though, that the Chinese use *ground* pork, to *season* the tofu, so the dish is light.

Having said that, make sure the ground pork you buy isn't too lean. You want a little fatty richness to add taste and suave texture to this lovely dish.

Serves 4

1 tablespoon grapeseed or canola oil
1 pound ground pork
$1/2$ cup scallions, white and green parts, cut $1/8$ inch thick
$1/3$ cup Black Bean–Garlic Sauce (page 32)
1 pound soft tofu, cut into $1/2$-inch dice
Kosher salt and freshly ground black pepper to taste

1. Heat a wok or large sauté pan over high heat. Add the oil and swirl to coat the pan. Add the pork and scallions and stir-fry, breaking up the pork, until the meat is cooked through, 5 to 6 minutes.

2. Add the Black Bean–Garlic Sauce and tofu and heat through, stirring gently to avoid breaking the tofu. Season with salt and pepper and serve immediately.

TRY IT

Put oysters, mussels, or clams on the half shell on a bed of salt, top each with a dollop of the sauce, and bake until just cooked.

For flavorful stuffing to use in chicken pinwheels or salami rolls, mix 1 part of the sauce with 2 parts of softened cream cheese.

The sauce is great tossed with pasta—or use it in baked potatoes in place of butter or other flavorings.

BLACK PEPPER–GARLIC SAUCE

This pungent, garlicky sauce owes its being to a famous crab and chile dish from Singapore. I wanted to concoct something similar using lobster, which is easier to eat than crab. With the help of a friend, Chris Yoh, I came up with the very dish, which has been a runaway hit ever since it was introduced at Blue Ginger. Its success made me realize that the sauce itself had a future.

Don't be alarmed by the amount of pepper in this. Once cooked, its heat is dissipated, so it doesn't blow your head off. What you get instead is a marvelous, elusive fragrance that perfectly complements the garlic.

Bring the sauce to room temperature and mix it well before you use it.

Makes about 3 cups
Lasts 1 month, refrigerated

1 tablespoon grapeseed or canola oil
20 garlic cloves, thinly sliced
1 cup scallions, white and green parts, cut ⅛ inch thick
1 heaping tablespoon medium-ground black pepper
2 cups dry white wine
2 cups Master Chicken Broth (page 192) or low-sodium canned chicken broth
2 tablespoons fish sauce (nam pla)
Juice of 1 lemon
8 tablespoons (1 stick) unsalted butter, cut into 1-tablespoon pieces

1. Heat a wok or large sauté pan over high heat. Add the oil and swirl to coat the pan. Add the garlic and stir-fry until soft, about 30 seconds. Add the scallions and black pepper, and stir. Add the wine, stock, fish sauce, and lemon juice and cook until the liquid is reduced by half, about 2 minutes.

2. Transfer the mixture to a blender and blend on high speed to purée. With the machine running, add the butter to form a creamy sauce. Use or store.

BEVERAGE TIP

Grape type
Gewürztraminer

Characteristics
Spicy, aromatic,
off-dry, lychee

Recommendations
Trimbach
Alsace, France

Gustave Lorentz
Alsace, France

OR

Grape type
Grenache, Shiraz,
Mourvedre

Characteristics
Velvety spice, ripe
berry, approachable

Recommendations
GSM Rosemount
McLaren Vale, Australia

Any Australian
sparkling Shiraz

BLUE GINGER BLACK PEPPER–GARLIC LOBSTER

This Blue Ginger standout is so simple to prepare and the peppery, garlicky sauce and lobster make one of those perfect culinary marriages; people can't get enough of it.

You'll need to break out the cleaver, or a heavy knife, to cut up the lobster. Can't swing lobster this week? Use shrimp instead. Butterfly them down the "back," keeping their shells as intact as you can, remove the sand veins, then proceed as the recipe directs, cooking them for about 3 minutes. Serve with rice or crusty bread to mop up the sauce.

Serves 4

2 tablespoons grapeseed or canola oil
3 1½- to 2-pound lobsters
½ cup dry white wine
2 cups Black Pepper–Garlic Sauce (page 40)
2 large tomatoes, cut into ½-inch dice
Juice of 1 lemon
2 scallions, green and white parts, cut ⅛ inch thick

1. With a cleaver or large, heavy knife, cut the tails from the lobsters' bodies. Twist off the claws and halve each lengthwise. Cut the tails along the joints into 4 or 5 sections.

2. Heat a wok or large sauté pan over high heat. Add the oil and swirl to coat the pan. Add half the lobster and stir-fry until the shells turn red, 3 to 4 minutes; remove and reserve. Repeat with the remaining lobster pieces. Return the reserved lobster to the wok and add the wine. Cook over high heat until the wine has reduced to 2 tablespoons, about 2 minutes. Add the Black Pepper–Garlic Sauce, tomatoes, and lemon juice, stir, and bring just to a simmer. Do not allow the mixture to boil or the sauce may break. Garnish with scallions and serve immediately.

PAN-SEARED SIRLOIN WITH MELTED BLACK PEPPER–GARLIC NAPA CABBAGE

Anyone who's tried steak au poivre—grilled steak coated with coarse peppercorns —knows how good that combo is. This dish features it in a sauce made with "melted" cabbage, a technique I learned in France. There, we'd make a cabbage fondue, which we served alongside the entrée; here, the cabbage, cooked to melting softness, lends delicious flavor and texture to the dish itself.

I like to use sirloin for this; it has got real oomph and is relatively cheap.

Serves 4

Four 8- to 10-ounce sirloin steaks, 1 to 1 $\frac{1}{2}$ inches thick
Kosher salt and freshly ground black pepper to taste
3 tablespoons grapeseed or canola oil
2 tablespoons Dijon mustard
1 large head of napa cabbage, halved, cored, and cut into $\frac{1}{4}$-inch slices
   (about 5 cups)
Juice of 1 lemon
1 cup Black Pepper–Garlic Sauce (page 40)

1. Season the steaks with salt and pepper.

2. Heat a large, heavy sauté pan over high heat. Add 2 tablespoons of the oil and swirl to coat the pan. Cook the steaks until done to taste, 4 to 5 minutes per side for medium-rare. Remove from the pan and rub with the mustard on all sides. Keep warm.

3. Reheat the pan over high heat. Add the remaining tablespoon of oil and swirl to coat the pan. Add the cabbage and stir-fry until very soft and lightly brown, 5 to 6 minutes. Season with salt and pepper. Add the lemon juice and Black Pepper–Garlic Sauce and heat thoroughly.

4. To serve, cut 3 or 4 slices at a 45-degree angle from each steak, leaving the rest of the meat intact. Arrange each steak on a dinner plate. Mound the cabbage on top of the steaks and pour its liquid around them.

TRY IT
Spread the sauce on
tortillas when serving
tacos or fajitas.

Use it as a dip for chicken
fingers or fish sticks.

Drizzle it over vegetable,
shrimp, or chicken
stir-fries.

HOISIN-LIME SAUCE

If you're like most people, your first encounter with hoisin sauce involved the Chinese dish mu shu pork, in which the sauce serves as a dipper for meat-enclosed pancakes. Used this way (and even *in* dishes), this bean-paste ingredient is too sweet, I find. That's why I came up with this sprightly lime-flavored version. The acidic kick of the lime bounces off the sauce's sweetness to create a delicious "new" hoisin. I've also added aromatics to the sauce to ensure it's well rounded— and versatile.

Makes about 2 cups
Lasts 2 weeks, refrigerated

$1/2$ cup plus 2 tablespoons grapeseed or canola oil
2 tablespoons minced garlic
1 tablespoon peeled and minced fresh ginger
2 cups hoisin sauce
$1/2$ cup fresh lime juice
Kosher salt and freshly ground black pepper to taste

1. Heat a wok or large sauté pan over medium heat. Add the 2 tablespoons of oil and swirl to coat the pan. Add the garlic and ginger and sauté until soft, about 2 minutes. Add the hoisin sauce and stir to prevent burning. Cook, stirring, for 1 minute, then add the lime juice.

2. Transfer the mixture to a blender and blend, drizzling in the $1/2$ cup oil. Season with salt and pepper. Cool thoroughly and use or store.

BEVERAGE TIP

Grape type
Chardonnay

Characteristics
Bright, tropical fruit,
slight butter

Recommendations
Byron Hangtime
Santa Maria Valley,
California

Grgich Hills
Napa Valley, California

Bouchard Père & Fils,
Pouilly-Fuisse
Burgundy, France

GRILLED HOISIN-LIME BARBECUED CHICKEN WITH ZUCCHINI

This is my down-home Asian version of barbecued chicken. The traditional American dish has lots of sweetness and, usually, some heat. I've cooled it on the sweetness front here, but amped up the heat with fiery sambal. The result, thanks also to the addition of sauce-marinated zucchini, pleases all.

Sweet barbecue sauces are prone to burning, so have a filled spray bottle near the grill to douse any flare-ups. I like to fill the bottle with beer instead of water; why not add flavor when you can?

Serves 4

2¼ cups Hoisin-Lime Sauce (page 46)
1 tablespoon sambal oelek or liquid hot sauce, or to taste
4 bone-in chicken thighs with skin
4 medium whole boneless chicken breasts with skin
½ cup white parts of scallions cut ⅛ inch thick, plus 2 tablespoons julienned
   or chopped green parts, for garnish (optional)
2 large zucchini, ends trimmed, halved lengthwise, and flat sides scored lightly
Kosher salt and freshly ground black pepper to taste

1. Two hours or up to 24 hours in advance (the longer, the better), combine 2 cups of the Hoisin-Lime Sauce and the sambal oelek in a medium nonreactive bowl. Add the chicken and scallion whites and toss well. Marinate, refrigerated, turning the chicken at least once. Thirty minutes before cooking, add the zucchini, and stir to coat well.

2. Prepare an outdoor grill and heat to hot, or preheat a large grill pan or the broiler. Spray the grill with nonstick spray or coat the grill pan with 1 tablespoon of grapeseed or canola oil. Remove the chicken from the marinade and grill or broil it, turning once, until the skin is brown and crispy and the juices run clear when the meat is pierced with a fork, 8 to 12 minutes for the breasts, 12 to 15 minutes for the thighs.

3. About 5 minutes after the chicken has begun to cook, add the zucchini and cook, turning once, until brown, about 8 minutes total. Transfer to a cutting board.

4. Slice the zucchini and chicken breasts on the diagonal and arrange on a serving platter with the whole thighs. Drizzle with the remaining Hoisin-Lime Sauce, and garnish with the scallion julienne, if using.

BEVERAGE TIP

Grape type

Pinot Noir

Characteristics

Concentrated black
cherry and raspberry,
balanced acid, rich

Recommendations

Hartford
Sonoma Coast,
California

Domaine Drouhin,
Willamette Valley,
Oregon

Louis Latour
Nuit St. Georges
Burgundy, France

MING'S TIP

Lots of fat will render
from the duck as it cooks.
Save it and use it to make
luscious scrambled eggs or
your favorite stir-fry.

HOISIN-ROASTED DUCK WITH SWEET POTATOES

Here's my easy version of the famed Peking Duck, a delicious dish that nonetheless takes lifetimes to prepare. This one-pot variation, which features sweet potatoes (wonderful with the duck), is much, much simpler to make, and you still get crispy skin, savory meat, and the hoisin-sauce "accompaniment," not to mention deliciously roasted sweets that have absorbed the tasty duck drippings.

Serves 3 to 4

One 5- to 6-pound duck, rinsed and dried, and visible fat removed
Kosher salt and freshly ground black pepper to taste
1$\frac{1}{2}$ cups Hoisin-Lime Sauce (page 46)
$\frac{1}{2}$ cup red wine
2 large onions, cut into $\frac{1}{4}$-inch slices
4 large sweet potatoes, washed and cut into 6 to 8 wedges each

1. Season the duck inside and out with salt and pepper. In a medium bowl, combine the Hoisin-Lime Sauce and the wine. Rub the duck generously with the mixture inside and out, and marinate in the mixture, refrigerated, for at least 2 hours and up to overnight.

2. Place a roasting pan in the oven and preheat the oven to 375°F.

3. Combine the onions and potatoes in a large bowl. Season with salt and pepper, and toss.

4. Open the oven and carefully spray the roasting pan with nonstick cooking spray. Place one potato wedge in the pan. The potato should sizzle; if not, remove it and continue to heat the pan. When the pan is very hot, add the potato mixture to the pan and place the duck on top, breast side up. Turn the pan back to front and roast until the duck is brown, 35 to 40 minutes. Tent the duck with foil and continue to roast until the duck is cooked through, or the legs are easily moved, 30 to 35 minutes more. Transfer the duck to a cutting board and let rest for 10 to 15 minutes.

5. Using a flat spatula, loosen the potato mixture from the pan and transfer to the center of a platter. Place the whole duck on the potatoes, breast side up, and carve at table. You may also carve the duck before serving, separating the leg-thighs from the wings, and slicing the breast.

BEVERAGE TIP
Beer

Characteristics
Amber, hoppy, malty

Recommendations
Sam Adams
Boston, Massachusetts

Bass Ale
England

Samuel Smith's Nut
Brown Ale
England

ASIAN SLOPPY JOES

As a kid I always looked forward to my mom's sloppy joes, which she made with hoisin sauce in place of tomatoes and onions. It really worked. So I salute her here with my own hoisin-sauce version, which sneaks some tomatoes back in for acidic balance, and includes jalapeño for a bit of heat. (Sorry, Mom!)

I also supplement the usual beef with ground pork—another bow to my Asian roots. It's a delicious variation, but feel free to use the traditional beef alone (just please make sure the ground beef has some fat in it, for flavor).

Serves 4 to 6

2 tablespoons grapeseed or canola oil
2 medium red onions, cut into 1/4-inch dice
1 cup celery cut into 1/4-inch dice
2 jalapeños, stemmed and minced, or 1 tablespoon sambal oelek or hot sauce
1 pound ground beef
1 pound ground pork
8 ounces chopped roma tomatoes, canned or fresh
1 1/2 cups Hoisin-Lime Sauce (page 46)
Kosher salt and freshly ground black pepper to taste
4 to 6 hamburger buns
1 head of iceberg lettuce, shredded

1. Heat a large deep, heavy saucepan over high heat. Add the oil and swirl to coat the pan. Add the onions, celery, and jalapeños and sauté until soft, about 2 minutes. Add the beef and pork and brown lightly, breaking up any clumps with a wooden spoon, about 5 minutes.

2. Add the tomatoes and the Hoisin-Lime Sauce and season with salt and pepper. Bring the mixture to a slow simmer and cook until cooked down and thickened enough to mound when ladled, 30 to 45 minutes.

3. Toast the buns and place a bottom half on each serving plate. Top with some of the lettuce, large scoops of the sloppy joe mixture, and more lettuce. Place the top buns over the contents and serve.

TRADITIONAL SPICY
SAMBAL

ROASTED PEPPER–
LEMONGRASS SAMBAL

GINGER–FUJI APPLE
CHUTNEY

CUCUMBER KIMCHEE

SPICY MANGO SALSA

TOMATO–KAFFIR LIME
SALSA

GREEN CURRY PASTE

SAMBALS, SALSAS, CHUTNEYS, AND PASTES

Unlike sauces, most of the flavorings in this chapter feature chopped ingredients so you get interesting mouthfeel as well as great taste. Here, however, I treat these "condiments" not as tableside add-to's, but as basic ingredients. Traditional Spicy Sambal, for example, adds fiery taste to Spicy Crab Cakes, the best ones you'll ever make, while fragrant-smoky Roasted Pepper–Lemongrass Sambal enlivens a great sandwich made with meaty portobellos.

A lot of chefs have "discovered" chutneys, but Ginger–Fuji Apple Chutney, made from fragrant Fuji apples, enhances the filling of easily made spicy potstickers and a sauce for sautéed pork chops served with maple-flavored sweet potatoes, an awesome cold-weather dish.

Similarly, my quickly made cucumber-based kimchee is added to the cooking liquid in Braised Kimchee Short Ribs, which gives the ribs great flavor.

I think of salsas as the new American ketchup. They're great at the table, but Spicy Mango Salsa and Tomato–Kaffir Lime Salsa give dishes like Scallion-Crusted Cod with Mango Salsa and Asian Lamb "Gyros" with Tomato–Kaffir Lime Tzatziki built-in taste.

Perhaps the world's oldest convenience food, curry paste has always been an "ad-in," but my version is brightened with basil and mint, so you get more than just heat. It flavors dishes like Green Curry Chicken Noodles and Grilled Green Curry–Marinated Salmon and Eggplant Steaks. Like the other flavor-bases in this chapter, once you have it, it's a ready-when-you-are dish-maker.

MASTER RECIPE

TRY IT
Mix the sambal with
ground beef to make a
zestier meat loaf.

Add it to leftovers for a
quick flavor boost.

Pep up Chinese and
other takeout.

TRADITIONAL SPICY SAMBAL

Chile pastes are the ketchup of the Asian table. As a kid, I would try to outdo my grandfather by slathering the Chinese version, *la jaio*, onto almost everything my mom served. (The Rice Krispies escaped.)

I take my inspiration for this garlicky, mouth-tingling version from Indonesia's sambal oelek (*sambal* means sauce; *oelek* refers to the chile content). You can buy it in jars, but the reason to make it is that your own is so much fresher tasting— and, of course, free of any unwanted additions, such as preservatives. Though the recipes that follow put the sauce to great use, I suggest you set this fiery condiment right on your table and enjoy it freely, as I do.

Be sure to wear kitchen gloves when you make sambal to protect your hands and eyes from stray chile heat.

Makes about 2 1/2 cups
Lasts 1 month, refrigerated

2 pounds dried red or fresh jalapeños, stemmed and chopped very roughly
10 fresh Thai chiles, or 1 tablespoon red pepper flakes
1 cup minced garlic
1/4 cup grapeseed or canola oil
2 cups rice wine vinegar
1 teaspoon sugar
2 teaspoons salt

1. In a medium saucepan, combine the jalapeños, Thai chiles, garlic, and oil and cook over low heat until the ingredients soften and blend, about 15 minutes. Add the vinegar and cook until reduced by half, 12 to 15 minutes.

2. Remove from the heat and add the sugar and salt. Cool to room temperature. Transfer the mixture to a food processor and pulse 3 or 4 times to chop to a salsa-like texture. Store in the refrigerator in a tightly sealed jar.

SPICY CRAB CAKES

These are crab cakes with a difference—a tantalizing addition of sambal. Not that the crab itself is overlooked. This sweetly delicious seafood really shines in these totally superior cakes.

You can buy containers of lump crabmeat at your fish store and some supermarkets; check the meat for stray bits of shell. Made bite-size, these cakes are great hors d'oeuvres or finger food.

Makes 8 cakes

2 tablespoons Traditional Spicy Sambal (page 56) or store-bought sambal
$1/2$ cup mayonnaise
2 tablespoons chopped chives
1 teaspoon honey
Juice of 1 lime
1 pound lump crabmeat, picked over for shells and cartilage
Kosher salt and freshly ground black pepper to taste
1 cup all-purpose flour, for dredging
3 extra-large eggs, lightly beaten
1 cup panko (Japanese bread crumbs) or regular unseasoned bread crumbs
2 tablespoons grapeseed or canola oil
8 ounces mixed greens (optional)

1. In a small bowl, combine half the sambal, half the mayonnaise, and half the chives. Mix well and set aside, refrigerated.

2. In a medium bowl, combine the remaining sambal and mayonnaise with the honey, lime juice, and crabmeat, and season with salt and pepper.

3. Using a $1/4$-cup measuring cup, scoop out 8 portions of the mixture and place them on a plate. Wet your hands and form each portion into a cake, packing it tightly.

4. Place the flour, eggs, and panko on 3 separate deep plates. (Pie plates work well.) Dredge the cakes in the flour, dip in the beaten egg, and then dredge with the panko.

5. Heat a large sauté pan over high heat. Add the oil and swirl to coat the pan. Add the cakes, and sear on both sides until brown and crisp, about 3 minutes per side. Drain on paper towels.

6. Make wide Z's with the reserved mayonnaise mixture on 4 serving plates. Divide the greens among the plates, if using. Place 2 cakes on each plate, garnish with the remaining chives, and add a dollop of the reserved flavored mayo.

BEVERAGE TIP

Grape type
Riesling

Characteristics
Off dry, lychee,
green apple

Recommendations
Marcel Deiss Riesling
Alsace, France

Dr. L, Riesling
Mosel-Saar-Ruwer,
Germany

BEVERAGE TIP

Grape type

Sauvignon Blanc

Characteristics

Bright, high citrus,
pineapple, passion fruit

Recommendations

Geisen
Marlborough,
New Zealand

Babich
Marlborough,
New Zealand

AVOCADO-STUFFED SPICY CRAB SALAD

This simple, summery dish of avocado halves filled with crabmeat shares many of the ingredients used in the preceding recipe. In fact, I think of it as a no-cooking variation (though, of course, the two dishes are different in approach). It makes a great dinner-party dish; just stuff the avocados, put them in the fridge on plates, and pull them out when you're ready to eat.

Serves 4

2 ripe Hass avocados
3 limes, 2 halved, 1 juiced
1 tablespoon Traditional Spicy Sambal (page 56) or store-bought sambal
¼ cup mayonnaise
2 tablespoons chopped chives
1 teaspoon honey
1 pound lump crabmeat, picked over for shells and cartilage
Kosher salt and freshly ground black pepper to taste
1 head of Boston lettuce (or other soft lettuce), separated into leaves, washed, and well dried

1. Halve the avocados, remove their pits, and, using a large spoon, separate the flesh from the skin, keeping the halves as intact as possible. (Discard the skin.) Coat the avocado halves all over with the lime juice, to prevent discoloration.

2. In a medium bowl, combine the sambal, mayonnaise, chives, honey, and crab-meat and mix. Season with salt and pepper.

3. Fill the avocado halves with the crab mixture. Serve atop the lettuce leaves and garnish each serving with a lime half.

BEVERAGE TIP

Grape type
Muscadet

Characteristics
Off dry, floral,
honeysuckle, slight
peach

Recommendations
Panther Creek Melon
Willamette Valley,
Oregon

Joao Pires, Muscat
Setúbal, Portugal

Sevres et Maines
Loire, France
(for a slight mineral
nose)

MY CRAZY CHICKEN–RICE NOODLE STIR-FRY

This is my take on a traditional Thai dish, known as crazy noodles. Why "crazy"? Because its spiciness leaves you goofy with delight.

Like other Southeast-Asian meat and noodle salads, this one is full of tempting flavors, but unlike most, it's easily prepared. In fact, you can fix it after work and have a light yet thoroughly satisfying chicken-and-noodle dish ready in minutes.

Serves 3 or 4

8 ounces transparent rice noodles (rice sticks)
2 tablespoons Thai fish sauce (nam pla)
2 tablespoons fresh lime juice
1 teaspoon sugar
1 tablespoon Traditional Spicy Sambal (page 56) or store-bought sambal
3 tablespoons grapeseed or canola oil
3 shallots, sliced 1/8 inch thick
1 pound ground chicken
1/2 cup scallions, green and white parts, sliced 1/8 inch thick
1/4 cup Thai or sweet basil leaves cut into 1/8-inch ribbons
1 lime, quartered, for garnish
4 sprigs of Thai or sweet basil for garnish

1. Fill a large bowl with warm water. Add the noodles and soak until tender, about 20 minutes. Drain and set aside.

2. Meanwhile, in a small bowl combine the fish sauce, lime juice, sugar, and sambal, and stir until the sugar is dissolved.

3. Heat a wok or large, heavy sauté pan over high heat. Add the oil and swirl to coat the pan. Add the shallots and stir-fry until brown, about 1 minute. Add the chicken and stir-fry, breaking up the meat, until cooked through, about 3 minutes. Add the noodles and sauce mixture and heat through, stirring. Add the scallions and basil ribbons and toss well. Garnish with the lime wedges and basil sprigs and serve immediately.

MASTER RECIPE

TRY IT
For a quick and tasty ceviche, combine 8 ounces of shrimp that you've cut into $1/2$-inch dice with $1/4$ cup of the sambal and the juice of 1 lemon. Marinate for 10 minutes, stirring occasionally, and serve in a chilled bowl with tortillas.

Make a spicy vinaigrette with 1 cup of the sambal, the juice of 2 lemons, and $1/2$ cup grapeseed oil. Toss with your favorite greens.

Great as a relish for hot dogs or other sausages.

MING'S TIP
To skin and add smoky flavor to bell peppers and jalapeños, blacken their surfaces uniformly, turning with tongs as necessary, over a burner flame or grill, or in the broiler. If working over a burner, hold the pepper using tongs, or, if large enough, rest the pepper on the burner grid. When evenly blackened, transfer the pepper to a bowl, cover with plastic wrap, and allow steam to loosen the skin. When the pepper is cool enough to handle, slide off the skin with your fingers, cut, and remove ribs and seeds.

ROASTED PEPPER–LEMONGRASS SAMBAL

Unlike Traditional Spicy Sambal (page 56), this is not knock-your-socks-off fiery, though it does have some heat. It *is* deliciously tart-sweet with an intriguing smokiness, due to the roasted peppers. I fell in love with roasted peppers on my first trip to Spain; these Western flavor-makers plus Eastern lemongrass yield an outstanding table condiment for your favorite seafood or meat dish—or use it as a "salsa" with tortilla chips.

Store this in a jar with a tight lid.

Makes 2 cups
Lasts 2 weeks, refrigerated

1 tablespoon grapeseed or canola oil
5 medium shallots, minced
5 stalks of lemongrass, white part only, minced
2 cups rice wine vinegar
10 medium red bell peppers, roasted (see Ming's Tip, left), peeled, seeded, and roughly chopped
2 red jalapeño chiles, roasted (see Ming's Tip, left), peeled, seeded, and cut into $1/8$-inch dice
Salt to taste

1. Heat a wok or heavy sauté pan over medium heat. Add the oil and swirl to coat the pan. Add the shallots and sauté until lightly browned, about 2 minutes. Add the lemongrass and sauté until soft, about 4 minutes. Add the vinegar, scrape the pan to deglaze it, then add the bell peppers and the jalapeños.

2. Reduce the heat to low, add the salt, and cook until the liquid has reduced by three quarters, 15 to 20 minutes. Remove the sambal from the heat and let it cool. Use or store.

GRILLED PORTOBELLO SANDWICH WITH ROASTED PEPPER–LEMONGRASS SAMBAL

I love a good sandwich. And I love steak. The two together should be the best, but steak sandwiches can be hit-and-miss. For this sandwich I've substituted meaty portobellos for steak to produce a quick, light feast that carnivores and veg-heads both love. With the tasty sambal as a "spread," it's also nearly fat-free, so it's healthier.

You can pack the sandwich and take it with you to work. Eat it with your favorite chips, and you're definitely in business.

Serves 4

1 tablespoon grapeseed or canola oil, if needed
4 large portobello mushrooms, stemmed and gills removed with a spoon
2 tablespoons extra-virgin olive oil
Kosher salt and freshly ground black pepper to taste
Juice of $1/2$ lemon
1 hothouse (seedless) cucumber, washed and cut diagonally into $1/8$-inch slices
4 kaiser rolls, halved and toasted
1 large tomato, sliced $1/8$ inch thick
About $1/4$ cup Roasted Pepper–Lemongrass Sambal (page 64)

1. Prepare an outdoor grill and heat to hot, or heat a grill pan or large sauté pan over high heat. Spray the grid well with nonstick spray or add the grapeseed oil to the pan and swirl to coat.

2. Rub the mushroom caps on both sides with 1 tablespoon of the olive oil and season with salt and pepper. Grill or sauté the caps, turning once, until softened, 4 to 5 minutes per side.

3. Stack the caps and let stand for 3 to 5 minutes. (This steams the caps to complete their cooking.) Unstack the caps and, angling a knife almost parallel to your cutting surface, cut them to make long, flat slices about $1/4$ inch thick.

4. In a medium bowl combine the remaining tablespoon of olive oil and the lemon juice. Add the cucumber, toss to coat, and season with salt and pepper.

5. Overlap the cucumber slices on the bottom halves of the rolls. Lay the mushroom slices (folded, if necessary) on top, followed by the tomato slices, and season again with salt and pepper. Top with a heaping tablespoon (or more if you wish) of the sambal. Top with the remaining roll halves, halve the sandwiches, and serve.

BEVERAGE TIP
Grape type
Mourvedre, Grenache
Rosé

Characteristics
Light and buttery, bell pepper, cranberry, tart balanced

Recommendations
Tavel Rosé
Rhone, France

Bandol Rosé
Bandol, France

BEVERAGE TIP

Grape type

Pinot Noir

Characteristics

Approachable,
light tannins and acid,
berry forward,
balanced finesse

Recommendations

A to Z
Willamette Valley,
Oregon

Iron Horse
Sonoma County,
California

Savigny-lés-Beaune
Burgundy, France

BRAISED CHICKEN WITH MUSHROOMS AND ROASTED PEPPER–LEMONGRASS SAMBAL

This warming dish is my Asian coq au vin. That French classic uses wine to add flavor and a nice tartness to chicken simmered with mushrooms and other good things. Here, the tartness comes from the sambal, which also adds spicy taste. I have very fond memories of dishes like this one, the kind that perfume the house with wonderful smells, so I recommend it as a cool-weather treat. I also suggest you double the recipe, as "leftovers" are even better the next day.

Serve this one with rice.

Serves 4

2 pounds bone-in chicken thighs, with skin
Kosher salt and freshly ground black pepper to taste
2 tablespoons grapeseed or canola oil
1 pound button mushrooms, sliced 1/4 inch thick
2 large onions, sliced 1/4 inch thick
4 cups Master Chicken Broth (page 192) or low-sodium canned chicken broth,
    plus additional, if needed
1 1/4 cups Roasted Pepper–Lemongrass Sambal (page 64)

1. Season the chicken with salt and pepper. Heat a heavy 2- to 3-quart saucepan or small stockpot over high heat. Add the oil and swirl to coat the pan. Add the chicken, skin side down, and sauté until brown, 6 to 8 minutes.

2. Turn the chicken, add the mushrooms and onions, and sauté until the vegetables are soft, about 5 minutes. Add the stock and 1 cup of the sambal. The liquid should cover the chicken; if not, add more stock. Correct the seasoning with salt and pepper. Bring to a simmer and cook, covered, until the chicken almost falls from the bone, 45 minutes to 1 hour. Place the chicken in pasta bowls and spoon 1 tablespoon of sambal over each serving. Serve with rice on the side.

BEVERAGE TIP
Grape type
Lambrusco

Characteristics
Easy drinking, fruity, dry

Recommendations
Villa di Corlo
Emilia-Romagna, Italy

Serve cold

ORZO WITH SAUSAGE AND ROASTED PEPPER–LEMONGRASS SAMBAL

Orzo is *the* East–West pasta: It's shaped like rice. This is my version of a traditional Italian sausage "fry," but one that's really more like a one-dish pilaf, as the sausage and orzo are cooked together with fennel, the sambal, and some wine. The savory result is homey but also distinctive; you can serve the dish out of the pan at table, or make it part of a buffet spread (it stays hot for 30 minutes or so).

This is easy to do and a real winner.

Serves 4

2 tablespoons grapeseed or canola oil
6 hot pork sausages, or hot or mild chicken or turkey sausages
2 cups raw orzo or other short pasta like ditalini
2 large onions, cut into 1/2-inch dice
1 large fennel bulb, cored and cut into 1/4-inch slices
1 cup white wine
1 1/4 cups Roasted Pepper–Lemongrass Sambal (page 64)
3 cups Master Chicken Broth (page 192) or low-sodium canned chicken broth
Kosher salt and freshly ground black pepper to taste

1. Heat a large, heavy sauté pan (with a lid) over high heat. Add the oil and swirl to coat the pan. Add the sausages and sauté, turning as needed, until well colored, about 8 minutes. Remove sausages and set aside.

2. Add the orzo and onions and sauté, stirring, until the onions are soft and the orzo is lightly toasted, 2 to 3 minutes. Season with salt and pepper.

3. Add the fennel and wine, scrape the pan to deglaze it, and cook until the wine is reduced by half, about 3 minutes. Add 1 cup of the sambal, the stock, and the sausages. Bring to a simmer, cover, and reduce the heat to low. Simmer until the orzo is cooked and all the liquid is absorbed, 30 to 40 minutes. Correct the seasoning with salt and pepper. Spoon over the remaining 1/4 cup of sambal and serve from the pan. Alternatively, divide the orzo among 4 plates, slice the sausages diagonally, and arrange them on the orzo. Spoon the remaining sambal over and serve.

MASTER RECIPE

TRY IT
This makes a terrific spread for a grilled ham and cheese sandwich.

Purée the chutney in a blender or food processor and use it as a dip for pork or duck satays.

Make a superior mince pie by filling a prebaked 10-inch pie shell (purchased is fine) with a mixture of 1½ cups diced cooked pork and 2 cups of the chutney. Bake until the filling is heated through, 30 to 40 minutes.

GINGER–FUJI APPLE CHUTNEY

Apples are, of course, great raw, but they're equally good, if not better, cooked. This tart-sweet chutney, spiked with ginger, takes advantage of the fact, and ups the taste ante by using fragrant Fuji apples. This wonderful apple provides subtly sweet flavor; it also keeps its shape when cooked, so the finished chutney has body. (If you can't get Fujis, any non-mealy apple can be substituted.) Chutneys are great, versatile condiments to have on hand, and this is one of the best.

Keep the chutney in the fridge. Its flavor will intensify with time.

Makes 4 cups
Lasts 1 week, refrigerated

4 cups Fuji or other non-mealy red apples (8 to 10 apples), peeled, cored, and cut into ¼-inch dice
Juice of 1 lemon
1 tablespoon grapeseed or canola oil
2 medium onions, cut into ¼-inch dice
2 tablespoons peeled and minced fresh ginger
Kosher salt and freshly ground black pepper to taste
1 cup rice wine vinegar
1 cup apple juice

1. In a large, nonreactive bowl, toss the apples with the lemon juice.

2. Heat a large, nonreactive saucepan over medium heat. Add the oil and swirl to coat the pan. Add the onions and ginger and sauté until the onions are soft, 3 to 4 minutes. Add the apples and cook, stirring gently, for 3 minutes. Season with salt and pepper.

3. Add the vinegar and apple juice and cook until the liquid is reduced by three quarters, about 30 minutes. Correct the seasoning and cool before ladling into a tightly sealed jar.

PORK AND GINGER–
FUJI APPLE CHUTNEY POT STICKERS

I've probably eaten more Chinese dumplings than anything else in my life. The reason's not hard to grasp for anyone who's enjoyed their taste and texture. Here's a true East–West pot sticker: The technique is traditional, but the sweet-tart filling is definitely and deliciously Western. With Ginger–Fuji Apple Chutney and store-bought wrappers on hand, all you have to do is fill and form the dumplings. The recipe is detailed, but once you make it, it's like riding a bike—it becomes second nature.

Just keep in mind that the seal is the most important aspect of dumpling making; it really doesn't matter how many folds you use to enclose the filling, or how gorgeous the result. As a kid, it was my job to form the dumplings, so you know it can't be *too* hard to master.

Makes 16 to 20 pot stickers

FILLING
1 pound ground pork
2 tablespoons soy sauce
1/2 cup scallions, white and green parts, sliced 1/8 inch thick
1 cup Ginger–Fuji Apple Chutney (page 72)
Kosher salt and freshly ground black pepper to taste

1 egg
1 package (50 count) round dumpling wrappers

2 tablespoons grapeseed or canola oil
Dim Sum Dipper (recipe follows)

1. To make the filling, fill a large bowl with ice. Set a medium bowl into the ice-filled bowl. In the smaller bowl combine the pork and soy sauce and mix. Fold in the scallions and chutney and season with salt and pepper.

2. To form the pot stickers, in a small bowl mix the egg with 2 tablespoons of water. Lay 5 wrappers on a work surface. Place 1/2 tablespoon of the filling in the center of each wrapper. Avoid getting any filling on the edges of the wrapper, which would prevent them from sealing properly. With a finger or pastry brush, paint the circumference of the wrappers with the egg mixture. Fold each wrapper in half to form a half-moon shape. Seal by pressing between the fingers and, starting at the center, make 3 pleats, working toward the bottom-right corner. Repeat, working toward the bottom-left corner. Press the folded edges of the dumplings gently on the work surface to flatten the bottoms and help them stand.

RECIPE CONTINUES

BEVERAGE TIP
Grape type:
Pinot Gris

Characteristics
Appley, melon and lemon zest notes, dry

Recommendations

Trimbach
Alsace, France

Chehalem Reserve
Willamette Valley, Oregon

MING'S TIPS
Dumpling wrappers are usually available in 1-pound packages, sold fresh or frozen. Labels usually indicate the kind of dumpling—potstickers, boiled dumplings, and so on—for which the skins are intended.

Cover wrappers you'll be using with a damp cloth to prevent them from drying out. Never use wrappers that have dried, even partially; they're liable to crack and cause leaks when the dumplings are cooked.

3. Heat a large, nonstick lidded sauté pan over high heat. Add the oil and swirl to coat the pan. When the oil is hot, add the pot stickers, flattened bottoms down, in batches of two or three rows of five, and cook without disturbing until brown, 3 to 4 minutes. Add about $1/2$ cup of water and immediately cover the pan to avoid splattering. Lift the cover and make sure about $1/8$ inch of water remains in the pan; add a little more if not. Steam until the pot stickers are puffy yet firm and the water has evaporated, 8 to 10 minutes. If the water evaporates before the pot stickers are done, add more in $1/4$-cup increments. If the pot stickers seem done, but water remains in the pan, drain it and return the pan to the stovetop to evaporate any remaining liquid.

4. Continue to cook over high heat to allow the pot stickers to recrisp on the bottom, 2 to 3 minutes. Be careful not to burn them. Transfer the pot stickers to a platter and serve with the dipping sauce in individual small ramekins.

DIM SUM DIPPER

This is a great dipping sauce for all dim sum—pot stickers, shu mai, spring rolls, scallion pancakes, to name a few—but it's also excellent with any fried goodie, like chicken fingers. You can and should adjust the heat to suit your palate. Though the dip lasts about a week in the fridge, it's so easily prepared that I recommend you make just as much as you need when you need it. In any case, always give diners their own servings in little bowls for individual dipping. That keeps everything sanitary and cuts down on the possibility of spoilage.

Makes about 1 cup

2 tablespoons Traditional Spicy Sambal (page 56) or store-bought sambal
$1/2$ cup rice wine vinegar
$1/2$ cup soy sauce
1 teaspoon sesame oil

In a small bowl combine the sambal, vinegar, soy sauce, and sesame oil. Mix and use or store.

BEVERAGE TIP
Grape type
Sauvignon Blanc

Characteristics
Balanced, rich, touch
of vanillin, explosive
citrus-pineapple

Recommendations
Didier Dagueneau
"Silex"
Pouilly-Fumé
Loire, France

MING'S TIP
As soon as the potatoes
are cooked, halve them.
Then, holding them in a
cloth-protected hand,
scoop the flesh into a
bowl and add *chilled*
butter. The hot spuds
and the cold butter
yield the fluffiest
result, as the butter
doesn't have a chance
to get oily.

SAUTÉED PORK CHOPS WITH GINGER–FUJI APPLE SAUCE AND MAPLE SWEET POTATOES

This is a great dish to serve when the weather turns cool: seared chops sauced with a chutney-flavored reduction, served with maple syrup–flavored mashed potatoes. You can probably tell how the dish evolved; the pork and apple combo is a Western classic, as is a mashed-potato accompaniment. I wanted to balance the sweetness of the apples, so I sweetened the potatoes a bit. This may sound contradictory, but it really works, and, moreover, it deepens all the flavors.

For extra juiciness, I recommend you brine the chops in cold salted water (it should taste as salty as seawater) for at least 30 minutes (and up to 4 hours) in the fridge before you cook them. Go light on the subsequent salt seasoning if the chops are brined. Wrapping the potatoes in foil helps cook them quicker—and don't worry about their being steamed, as we're not looking for a mealy result here.

Serves 4

4 medium sweet potatoes
¼ cup pure maple syrup
2 to 4 tablespoons cold unsalted butter, as desired, plus 1 tablespoon
Kosher salt and freshly ground black pepper to taste
4 ½-inch-thick loin pork chops
1 cup all-purpose flour
2 tablespoons grapeseed or canola oil
1 cup Master Chicken Broth (page 192) or low-sodium canned chicken broth
1 cup white wine
1½ cups Ginger–Fuji Apple Chutney (page 72)
¼ cup chopped fresh flat-leaf parsley

1. Preheat the oven to 400°F.

2. Wrap each potato in aluminum foil and bake until a knife can pierce the potatoes easily, 30 to 40 minutes. As soon as the potatoes are cool enough to handle, scoop out the flesh and transfer it to a bowl. Use a heavy whisk to whip

RECIPE CONTINUES

the potatoes. Add the maple syrup and 2 to 4 tablespoons of the butter, whisk to blend, and season with salt and pepper. Cover with foil to help keep the potatoes warm and set aside. Don't turn off the oven.

3. Season the chops on both sides with salt and pepper and dredge in the flour. Heat a large, heavy, ovenproof sauté pan over high heat. Add the oil and swirl to coat. Add the chops and sear on one side until brown, 3 to 4 minutes. Turn the chops and transfer to the oven. Bake the chops until medium done, 8 to 10 minutes. Turn off the oven.

4. Transfer the chops to a heat-proof plate and allow to rest for 5 minutes. Place the sauté pan over high heat, add the broth and wine, and deglaze the pan, scraping to incorporate any browned bits. Reduce the liquid by half, about 4 minutes, and add the chutney and the remaining tablespoon of butter. Add the parsley and correct the seasoning.

5. Place small mounds of the potatoes on serving plates. Place a chop on each mound, pour the sauce over, and serve.

POTATO PANCAKES WITH APPLE-SCALLION CREAM

This is dedicated to my co-author, Arthur Boehm, and his mom, both of whom have seen many potato pancakes in their day. (Artie says his mom's are the best, but read on.) My first encounter with latkes was at a bar mitzvah in my hometown of Dayton, Ohio. I ate eight, almost in a gulp. I was embarrassed, but I resolved to make potato pancakes a part of my life from that moment on. This super version, accompanied by irresistible apple scallion cream, is the fruit of that decision.

Once the potatoes are grated, they'll begin to brown, due to oxidation, so work quickly. (The browning doesn't really affect their taste, but it can make the finished pancakes unsightly.) And, if my experience is any indication, make plenty.

Serves 4

1 cup Ginger–Fuji Apple Chutney (page 72)
1 cup sour cream
4 scallions, white and green parts separated and coarsely chopped
4 large russet potatoes, peeled
2 eggs, lightly beaten
Kosher salt and freshly ground black pepper to taste
2 tablespoons unsalted butter
2 tablespoons grapeseed or canola oil

1. To make the apple-scallion cream, combine the chutney, sour cream and all but 1 tablespoon of the scallion greens in a small bowl and mix. (Reserve the remaining greens for garnish.) Refrigerate if not using immediately.

2. Using a food processor with a coarse grating disk, or the coarse side of a box grater, grate the potatoes. Transfer the potatoes to a large strainer set over a bowl and use a large spoon to gently press down on the potatoes to remove as much liquid as possible. In a large bowl, combine the potatoes, eggs, and the scallion whites. Season to taste with the salt and pepper.

3. Heat half the butter and half the oil in each of 2 large nonstick pans over medium heat (or work in 2 batches with 1 pan). Add ⅓ cup of the potato mixture for each pancake, flattening it to make 4 to 6 pancakes about 4 inches in diameter. Cook until the bottoms of the pancakes are brown, 3 to 4 minutes. Turn the pancakes and repeat. (If using 1 pan, keep the first batch warm in a 200°F. oven while you prepare the second.) Dollop with the apple-scallion cream, garnish with the remaining scallion greens, and serve.

BEVERAGE TIP
Grape type
Chenin Blanc

Characteristics
Toasted yeast, lemon/lime notes, great value!

Recommendations
Chateau Montcontour
Loire, France

MING'S TIP
If not using the apple scallion cream right away, store it in the fridge.

MASTER RECIPE

CUCUMBER KIMCHEE

Kimchee is the spicy pickle served with almost every Korean meal. It's usually made with fermented cabbage or turnip, and stored in a tightly sealed jar, it lasts forever. My cucumber version is equally spicy and has the added flavor of fresh ginger. The traditional method involves burying the kimchee to ferment it. You won't have to dig up the kitchen, however, as I use vinegar to do the same job.

I call for the traditional Korean chile, *kucho karu,* to make this, but you can just as effectively substitute regular red pepper flakes (and feel free to adjust the amount). Also, be very careful about putting unprotected fingers into the mixture, as you can too easily rub your eyes with them—not a good thing. Instead, use clean tongs or chopsticks to serve or transfer the kimchee.

Makes 6 cups
Lasts 2 weeks, refrigerated

6 medium cucumbers, halved lengthwise, and seeded
Kosher salt
6 cups rice wine vinegar
2 cups sugar
10 garlic cloves, thinly sliced
1/4 cup fresh ginger matchsticks (see Ming's Tip, left)
3 medium red onions, halved and cut into 1/8-inch slices
1 cup shredded carrots
4 tablespoons Korean chile flakes (kucho karu), or 2 tablespoons red pepper flakes
1/2 cup Thai fish sauce (nam pla)

1. Place the cucumbers in a colander set in the sink. Sprinkle the cut side of the cucumbers generously with the salt. Allow to rest at room temperature until the cucumbers have exuded liquid, about 2 hours. Rinse the cucumbers, dry them well, and slice them into 1/4-inch-thick half moons. Set aside.

2. In a large, nonreactive saucepan, combine the vinegar and sugar and bring to a boil over medium heat. Add the garlic, ginger, and onions, bring to a simmer, and remove immediately from the heat.

3. In a large, nonreactive bowl, combine the cucumbers and carrots. Pour the vinegar mixture over them, add the chile flakes and fish sauce, and toss well.

4. Correct the seasoning with salt. Let the mixture cool to room temperature and cover with plastic wrap. With a paring knife, punch a few holes in the plastic wrap and place the bowl in a cool, dark place. Let the mixture pickle for 24 hours. Transfer the kimchee to a tall glass jar or jars and seal tightly. Use or refrigerate.

TRY IT

This is a great sandwich or burger accompaniment. Use it as you would any pickle.

For a Korean tartar sauce, mix 1/2 cup of chopped kimchee with the same amount of mayo. Delicious as a dip for fried seafood.

Mix 1 cup of chopped kimchee with the juice of 2 lemons and 1/2 cup grapeseed oil. Toss this terrific vinaigrette with roasted vegetables or your favorite greens.

MING'S TIP

To make ginger matchsticks, first slice a peeled 1-inch-long piece of ginger horizontally into slices about 1/8 inch thick. Stack these and cut them vertically into 1/8-inch-wide sticks.

MING'S TIP

Kucho Karo is a traditional Korean hot red pepper powder that is hot (very hot), flavorful, and slightly sweet. Three kinds are available: fine- and coarse-ground, and flake, which is similar to Western hot pepper flakes. I find coarse-ground easiest to work with.

BEVERAGE TIP

Grape type

Shiraz

Characteristics

Red cherry, mint,
chocolate, cedar hints,
complex, balanced
tannins

Recommendations

Brokenwood, Shiraz
McLaren Vale, Australia

BRAISED KIMCHEE SHORT RIBS

Braised short ribs is a delicious cool-weather dish. But many versions lack flavor, due to an insipid braising liquid. As that liquid goes, so goes the dish, so here we're making sure it's really tasty by adding cucumber kimchee. That gives an irresistible spicy tartness to the finished ribs (plus the kimchee's acid helps cook them more quickly).

Serve this hearty dish family-style with bowls of hot rice. Pass additional kimchee, if you like, for even more spiciness.

Serves 4

3 pounds beef short ribs, cut into 3- to 4-inch pieces (have the butcher do this)
Kosher salt and freshly ground black pepper to taste
3 tablespoons grapeseed or canola oil
3 medium onions, cut into 2-inch dice
3 cups Cucumber Kimchee (page 82) with 1½ cups of its liquid, plus additional kimchee for garnish
One 1-pound bag of peeled baby carrots
4 large russet potatoes, cut into 2-inch dice
Kucho karu (Korean chile) for garnish (optional)

1. Season the short ribs with salt and pepper.

2. Heat a large Dutch oven or large, heavy stockpot over high heat. Add 2 tablespoons of the oil and swirl to coat the pan. Add the ribs and brown on all sides, 8 to 10 minutes.

3. Remove the ribs and wipe the pan with paper towels. Heat the pot over high heat and add the remaining tablespoon of oil. Swirl to coat the pan, add the onions, and sauté until they are soft, about 5 minutes. Add the kimchee liquid and cook until reduced by half, 6 to 8 minutes.

4. Return the ribs to the pot. Add the kimchee and enough water to cover the ribs and bring to a simmer. Season with salt and pepper. Cover with the lid slightly ajar and simmer until the meat is very tender, about 3 hours. During the last 30 minutes of cooking add the carrots and potatoes, and cook until tender. Use a slotted spoon to transfer the short ribs and vegetables to pasta bowls. Garnish with additional kimchee and chile, if using. Ladle some of the broth over each portion and serve.

BEVERAGE TIP

Grape type

Sauvignon Blanc

Characteristics

Lime citrus integrated,
vanilla, toasted cream

Recommendations

Artesa

Napa Valley, California

Matanzas Creek

Sonoma Valley,
California

KIMCHEE "CHOUCROUTE" WITH SEARED DIJON HALIBUT

Most cooks know that choucroute garni is an Alsatian dish consisting of braised, tart cabbage (like our sauerkraut) garnished with meats including sliced pork and sausage. Served with sharp mustard, it's a hearty feast, though a bit heavy for today's tastes. An attempt to lighten the dish, and my love of all things hot-hot, led me to devise this tart-spicy seafood version, which everyone loves.

As elsewhere, the addition of the cucumber kimchee adds a spicy Eastern note; and this time, mustard is used to coat the fillets before they're seared for cooked-in flavor.

Serves 4

1/4 cup grapeseed or canola oil
2 large heads of cabbage, cored, halved, and cut into 1/4-inch ribbons
Kosher salt and freshly ground black pepper to taste
3 cups Cucumber Kimchee (page 82), plus additional, with 1 1/2 cups
  of its liquid
1 bottle dry white wine
1 bay leaf
4 halibut fillets, 6 to 7 ounces each
4 tablespoons Dijon mustard

1. Heat a large sauté pan or deep heat-proof casserole over high heat. Add 2 tablespoons of the oil and swirl to coat the pan. Add the cabbage, season with salt and pepper, and cook, stirring, until soft but not colored, 5 to 8 minutes.

2. Add the kimchee liquid and the wine and reduce the mixture by three quarters, 20 to 30 minutes. Add the 3 cups of kimchee and the bay leaf and simmer until the cabbage has almost melted, 30 to 40 minutes.

3. About 20 minutes before you are ready to serve, heat the oven to 425°F. Season the halibut with salt and pepper. Heat a large ovenproof sauté pan, preferably nonstick, over high heat until hot. Add the remaining two tablespoons of oil and swirl to coat the pan. Add the fish and sear until brown, about 4 minutes. Turn the fillets, rub the mustard on the cooked sides, and transfer the pan to the oven. Bake until the fish is cooked through and flaky, 4 to 6 minutes. Divide the "choucroute" among 4 pasta bowls, discarding the bay leaf. Place the fillets on it, garnish with the additional kimchee, and serve.

BEVERAGE TIP

Grape type

Riesling

Characteristics

Off dry, lychee, wet
stone, appley

Recommendations

Domaine Schlumberger
Alsace, France

Eroica
Columbia Valley,
Washington State

SPICY KIMCHEE, PORK, AND TOFU BRAISE

This is based on one of my favorite Korean dishes, braised sliced tofu served with kimchee. My contribution is the use of kimchee *in* the dish, which adds delicious, spicy flavor. Although this is made with pork (ground, so it's more of a seasoning), it can also be prepared with chicken or without any meat at all. This is so simple to put together, and so tasty, that you really owe it to yourself to give it a try. Serve it with white rice.

Serves 4

1 tablespoon grapeseed or canola oil
1 pound ground pork
1 pound baby spinach, rinsed and dried
1 pound firm tofu, cut into 1/2-inch dice
2 cups Cucumber Kimchee (page 82), strained
Kosher salt and freshly ground black pepper to taste
Sesame oil, for drizzling

1. Heat a large wok or sauté pan over high heat. Add the oil and swirl to coat the pan. Add the pork and cook, stirring to break up the meat, until the pork is just cooked through, about 5 minutes.

2. Add the spinach, tofu, and kimchee and toss gently to mix. Season with salt and pepper. Heat the vegetables through thoroughly, transfer to a serving plate, and drizzle with sesame oil. Serve immediately.

BEVERAGE TIP
Grape type
Chardonnay and
Pinot Noir

Characteristics
Ripe berry flavors,
toasty, yeasty, bright
acid and fine mousse

Recommendations
Pacific Echo Brut Rosé
Anderson Valley,
California

SPICY CUCUMBER-KIMCHEE RICE-NOODLE SOUP

This light but spicy soup gives you a taste of Korean cooking, and it's healthful. I make it with chicken broth, but you can vary its taste by using vegetable broth or even dashi, if you like.

For a nice addition, you can cook julienned raw chicken breast in the soup before serving it. Simmer the chicken until it's just cooked through, about 3 minutes. I also recommend you add a little additional Cucumber Kimchee to the soup just before its served.

Serves 4

8 ounces rice noodles
1 1/2 quarts Master Chicken Broth (page 192), or store-bought low-sodium
    chicken broth
2 cups Cucumber Kimchee (page 82)
Kosher salt and freshly ground black pepper to taste
4 cups shredded romaine lettuce leaves

1. In a medium bowl combine the noodles with enough hot tap water to cover them by 1 inch. Allow the noodles to soften, about 8 minutes. Drain the noodles and set aside.

2. In a large saucepan, bring the stock to a boil over high heat. Add the noodles and kimchee, allow the broth to return to a boil, and season with the salt and pepper.

3. Divide the romaine among 4 soup bowls. Ladle over the soup and serve.

MASTER RECIPE

TRY IT
Use the salsa as you would any other—as a dip with chips, with burritos, and so on.

Great as a condiment for grilled meats and fish, curries, and other spicy stews.

For a big flavor lift, add the salsa to black bean soup before serving it.

MING'S TIPS
To dice the mango, first cut the fruit horizontally on both sides of the pit. (Reserve the remaining piece with the pit.) Using a large tablespoon, scoop the flesh from the skin of both halves. Keeping the slices stacked, slice the flesh horizontally, then cut vertically through the stack to dice the flesh. Cut the flesh from the pit on the remaining piece and, as best you can, repeat the dicing procedure. As this can be tricky, I often buy an extra mango to get a whole mango's worth of diced flesh; whatever "extra" mango is left I eat.

To extract maximum juice from a lime or lemon, first roll the fruit under your palm on a hard surface.

SPICY MANGO SALSA

I'm a huge fan of salsa—and this mango salsa has to be at the top of my list. Sweet, fragrant mango is a perfect match for the heat of sambal, and ginger adds a second spicy layer.

As a mango lover from way back—when I was thirteen, visiting Taipei, I'd eat a mango a day, at four cents per fruit—I can tell you that there's no trick to buying them if you let your nose be your guide. Choose mangos that smell fragrant and sweet, and you'll be rewarded with delicious eating. (Color's not a reliable guide; even green mangos can be perfectly ripe.) The mango should also yield slightly to the touch.

Makes 6 cups
Lasts 1 to 1½ weeks, refrigerated

5 large, ripe mangos, peeled and cut into ¼-inch dice
2 medium red onions, cut into ¼-inch dice
2 red jalapeños, stemmed and minced
1 tablespoon peeled and minced fresh ginger
2 tablespoons Traditional Spicy Sambal (page 56) or store-bought sambal or hot pepper sauce
⅓ cup fresh lime juice (from 6 to 8 limes)
Kosher salt and freshly ground black pepper to taste

In a large, nonreactive bowl, combine the mangos, onions, jalapeños, ginger, sambal, and lime juice, and blend gently. Season with salt and pepper. Use or refrigerate.

BEVERAGE TIP

Grape type
Sauvignon Blanc

Characteristics
Mango, passion fruit,
pineapple,
tart and balanced

Recommendations
Babich,
Marlborough,
New Zealand

Mulderbosch
Stellenbosch,
South Africa

SCALLION-CRUSTED COD WITH MANGO SALSA

Cod is one of my favorite fish. Mild and flaky, it has a deliciously sweet, fresh-from-the-sea flavor. That natural sweetness is accented by the mango salsa, which also adds tantalizing heat.

I like to use panko, Japanese bread crumbs, to dredge the cod fillets before sautéing them, but any fine, unflavored bread crumbs will do.

Serves 4

4 skinned cod fillets, preferably center-cut, 6 to 8 ounces each
Kosher salt and freshly ground black pepper to taste
2 cups panko (Japanese bread crumbs) or regular bread crumbs
1/2 cup thinly sliced scallions
1 egg lightly beaten with 1 tablespoon water
2 tablespoons grapeseed or canola oil
1 cup Spicy Mango Salsa (page 90)
1/4 cup chopped fresh cilantro

1. Preheat the oven to 400°F.

2. Season the cod on both sides with salt and pepper. On a large plate, combine the panko and scallions. Using a pastry brush, lightly brush the fillets with the egg wash and dredge in the panko on both sides.

3. Heat a large sauté pan over medium heat. Add the oil and swirl to coat the pan. Add the cod and sauté until the underside is brown, 3 to 4 minutes. Gently turn the fillets and transfer the pan to the oven. Bake until the fish is cooked through, 6 to 8 minutes.

4. Meanwhile, in a small bowl combine the salsa and the cilantro and mix. Dollop the salsa mixture onto 4 plates. Place the cod portions on top of the salsa and serve.

BEVERAGE TIP

Grape type
Pinot Grigio

Characteristics
Ripe melon-pear, hints
of the tropics, balanced
acid, fresh figs,
hint of ginger

Recommendations
Luna
Napa Valley, California

MING'S TIP

Make sure to salt the
water in which you blanch
the peas. The salt helps
the peas hold their color.
To test the peas for
doneness, taste one; they
should be cooked only
enough to remove the
raw flavor.

MANGO CHICKEN STIR-FRY WITH SNAP PEAS

Most people think mangos are only eaten raw, but they're also delicious cooked, as in this delicious stir-fry. When cooked, the fruit begins to break down and become caramely—absolutely wonderful when combined with seared chicken and crunchy snap peas.

Serve this with rice. And should there be any left over, it's great the next day, even straight from the fridge. In fact, I almost prefer it that way, as the flavors have had a chance to meld.

Serves 4

Kosher salt
1 pound snap peas, ends trimmed, if needed
2 pounds boneless, skinless chicken thighs, cut into 1-inch pieces
1 tablespoon Asian sesame oil
1 tablespoon cornstarch
1 tablespoon soy sauce
2 tablespoons grapeseed or canola oil
2 cups Spicy Mango Salsa (page 90)
Freshly ground black pepper to taste

1. Fill a large bowl with water and add ice. Bring a large pot of salted water to a boil and add the snap peas. Blanch until they brighten and have lost their raw taste, 1 to 2 minutes. Drain the snap peas and transfer them to the ice water. When cold, drain.

2. In a large bowl, combine the chicken, sesame oil, cornstarch, and soy sauce and mix. Set aside for 10 minutes.

3. Heat a wok or heavy sauté pan over high heat. Add the grapeseed oil and swirl to coat the pan. Add the chicken and stir-fry until just cooked through, 6 to 8 minutes. Add the snap peas and the salsa. Season with salt and pepper and serve.

BEEF AND SHIITAKE SATAYS WITH MANGO SAUCE

There's nothing better for satays than a great dipping sauce, and this delicious beef and shiitake version really *goes* with sweet-and-spicy mango salsa. You can prepare satays with just about anything: meat, seafood, and vegetables, alone or combined. The only key to success is making sure the various ingredients are cut so that they'll all be done at the same time.

You'll need four 4- to 5-inch wooden skewers for this, soaked in water for 20 minutes so they won't burn when grilled.

Serves 4

1 1/2 pounds flank steak, cut diagonally against the grain into strips 4 inches
   long and 1/4 inch thick
1 pound fresh shiitake mushrooms, stemmed and caps halved
1 bunch of scallions, white and green parts, cut into 2-inch lengths
1/4 cup soy sauce
1/3 cup red wine
1 tablespoon sugar
3/4 cup grapeseed or canola oil, plus 2 tablespoons for cooking, if needed
1 teaspoon coarsely ground black pepper, plus additional to taste
2 cups Spicy Mango Salsa (page 90)
Kosher salt to taste
2 ripe mangos, halved (see page 90), for garnish (optional)

1. In a large bowl, combine the flank steak, shiitakes, scallions, soy sauce, red wine, sugar, 1/4 cup of the oil, and the teaspoon of coarsely ground black pepper. Set aside for 30 minutes.

2. Meanwhile, in a blender, blend the salsa at high speed and drizzle in the remaining 1/2 cup of oil. Season with salt and pepper. Set aside.

3. To make the satays, thread each skewer with a length of scallion, either white or green part, a shiitake half, a strip of flank steak secured in an "S" shape, a second piece of shiitake, and a second scallion length. They should touch fairly tightly.

4. Prepare an outdoor grill and heat to hot, or preheat a grill pan or heavy sauté pan over high heat. Spray the grill grid with nonstick cooking spray, or add the 2 tablespoons of oil to the grill pan or sauté pan and swirl to coat. Cook the satays until the meat is medium-rare, turning once, 2 to 3 minutes per side.

5. Transfer the dipping sauce to an attractive bowl, arrange the satays on a platter, and serve with the sauce.

BEVERAGE TIP

Grape type
Merlot

Characteristics
Ripe plum, soft cocoa, supple tannins

Recommendations
Casa Lapostolle, Cuvée Alexander Colchagua Valley, Chile

MING'S TIPS

For a striking presentation, zigzag 4 plates with the mango mixture, place a mango half, rounded side up, on top, and stick the satays into the mango halves like pins in a pincushion.

For a more substantial snack, I wrap the satays in noodle-filled red lettuce leaves. Soak one 8-ounce package of rice or mung-bean noodles in hot water until they're soft, about 30 minutes; drain the noodles well. Divide the noodles among 4 red lettuce leaves, place a satay over each noodle portion, and pull out the skewers. Roll the satays in the leaves and serve with the dipping sauce.

MASTER RECIPE

TRY IT

As with all salsas, this one's terrific as a dip with chips, crudités, and so on. Serve it with grilled fish, too.

Dribble the salsa onto a composed salad (one made with ingredients that are arranged rather than tossed).

For a tasty, couldn't-be-easier vinaigrette, purée the salsa in a blender.

TOMATO–KAFFIR LIME SALSA

One of the most common salsa ingredients is lime juice, which gives the mixture a special zest. For this version, I've kicked things up by using incredibly fragrant kaffir lime leaves. This characteristic Thai ingredient gives this salsa super flavor, and it is also fiery enough for most chile heads.

Legend says that washing your hair in kaffir lime juice wards off evil spirits. Be that as it may, make sure you buy the leaves fresh, if you can, otherwise frozen.

Makes 8 cups
Lasts 2 weeks, refrigerated

6 large, ripe tomatoes cut into $1/2$-iinch dice
2 medium red onions, cut into $1/4$-inch dice
12 kaffir lime leaves, stemmed and minced, or the grated zest of 3 limes
Juice of 6 limes
$1/4$ cup soy sauce
3 red jalapeño chiles or 4 serrano chiles, stemmed and minced
$1/2$ cup extra-virgin olive oil
Kosher salt and freshly ground black pepper to taste

In a large, nonreactive bowl, combine the tomatoes, onions, kaffir lime leaves, lime juice, soy sauce, jalapeños, and olive oil and mix gently. Season with salt and pepper. Use or store.

BEVERAGE TIP

Grape type
Gamay

Characteristics
Clean, lightly roasted
red berry, spice nuance

Recommendations
Cru classè wines from
Morgon or Brouilly in
Beaujolais, France

Chateau de Pizay
Beaujolais, France

Desvignes
Beaujolais, France

Serve slightly chilled

ASIAN LAMB "GYROS" WITH TOMATO–KAFFIR LIME TZATZIKI

This dish reflects my love of Greek gyros—vertically roasted minced lamb molded around a giant spit—and particularly their cucumber–yogurt accompaniment. This simplified version of that sauce contains piquant salsa rather than the traditional garlic. And there's no need for a spit, as the meat's formed into quickly sautéed "sausages" that are encased in pita with shredded romaine. The result, when you eat it, is messy hands—and a party in your mouth.

Serves 4

1½ pounds ground lamb
1 small onion, minced
2 tablespoons minced fresh flat-leaf parsley
1 teaspoon freshly ground black pepper, plus additional to taste
3 tablespoons extra-virgin olive oil
1 cup Tomato–Kaffir Lime Salsa (page 98)
1 cup yogurt
1 small hothouse (seedless) cucumber, washed and cut into ¼-inch dice
Kosher salt
4 pita breads
1 cup romaine lettuce cut into ⅛-inch-wide ribbons

1. In a large bowl, combine the lamb, onion, parsley, the 1 teaspoon of pepper, and 2 tablespoons of the oil and mix well. With your hands, form the mixture into four "sausages" 6 inches long by about 1½ inches thick. Let them rest in the refrigerator for 30 minutes.

2. Meanwhile, in a small bowl, combine the salsa, yogurt, and cucumber. Season with salt and additional pepper to taste and set aside.

3. Heat a large sauté pan over high heat. Add the remaining 1 tablespoon oil and swirl to coat the pan. Add the lamb sausages and sauté them on all sides until brown on the outside and medium-rare inside, 6 to 8 minutes. Remove from the pan and let rest for 4 to 5 minutes.

4. Meanwhile, wipe out the pan. Working in batches, add the pitas and toast them lightly, about 30 seconds on each side.

5. To make the gyros, divide the romaine among the pitas. Add a lamb sausage, dollop on some sauce, and fold the gyro in half. Serve.

BEVERAGE TIP

Grape type

Chardonnay

Characteristics

Vanillin oak, peach, passion fruit, orange

Recommendations

Newton Unfiltered Napa Valley, California

MING'S TIP

Make sure to toss the burgers lightly from hand to hand as you form them. This eliminates air pockets so the burgers stay intact when cooked.

SALMON BURGER WITH TOMATO–KAFFIR LIME SALSA

This delicious fish is also one of the healthiest for us, due to its relatively abundant omega-3 oil content. Made into patties and served on buns with a tempting salsa, it's also fun to eat.

Yes, the salmon is mixed with butter before being formed into burgers. Butter adds richness, but you can omit it if you like without any harm.

Serves 4

1$\frac{1}{2}$ pounds skinless salmon fillet, cut into 1-inch dice
2 tablespoons cold unsalted butter, chopped into small pieces
Juice and minced zest of 1 lime
Kosher salt and freshly ground black pepper to taste
2 tablespoons grapeseed or canola oil, if needed
4 sesame seed buns, split and toasted
2 cups shredded romaine lettuce
1 cup Tomato–Kaffir Lime Salsa (page 98)

1. Prepare an outdoor grill and heat to hot. Alternatively, when ready to make the burgers, heat a large, heavy sauté pan over high heat.

2. In a food processor, pulse the salmon to grind it coarsely. Add the butter and pulse only enough to reduce the butter to very small pieces, 3 or 4 times.

3. Transfer the salmon to a large bowl and mix in the lime zest and juice. Make 4 patties, throwing the salmon back and forth between your hands as you work to eliminate any air pockets, and season with salt and pepper.

4. If using a sauté pan, add the oil to the pan and swirl to coat. Grill or sauté the burgers, turning once, until done, 4 minutes per side for medium-rare. Place the lettuce on the bun bottoms. Add the burgers, cover generously with the salsa, and top with the remaining bun halves. Serve.

BEVERAGE TIP

Wine Spritzer

Recommendations
With day-old leftovers,
hopefully pumped, of a
Viognier or Sauvignon
Blanc, mix 50/50 with
San Pellegrino, juice of
$1/2$ lime on ice.

MING'S TIP

For variety, you can
substitute spinach- or
chile-flavored tortillas
for the "regular" kind.

TOFU-MUSHROOM QUESADILLA WITH TOMATO–KAFFIR LIME SALSA

I got the idea for these delicious, cheeseless quesadillas from a traditional Chinese dish, braised tofu with shiitakes. The two make an inspired combination, so why not create an East–West version by wrapping them in tortillas with Tomato–Kaffir Lime Salsa? The tofu, used as is, gives you all the satisfying texture of cheese without the gooeyness or the calories, and the other ingredients do the rest.

This also makes great finger food for a party. Just slice the wrapped ingredients thin and arrange on a plate. And don't be alarmed if some of the filling falls out when you bite into the quesadillas; that's what eating them is about.

Serves 4

2 tablespoons extra-virgin olive oil
$1/2$ pound button mushrooms
Kosher salt and freshly ground black pepper to taste
1 red onion, sliced $1/8$ inch thick
2 cups Tomato–Kaffir Lime Salsa (page 98)
1 tablespoon minced fresh cilantro (optional)
2 tablespoons grapeseed or canola oil, if needed
4 to 6 large wheat tortillas
1 package silken tofu, cut lengthwise into $1/4$-inch-thick slices

1. Heat a wok or large sauté pan over high heat. Add the olive oil and swirl to coat the pan. Add the mushrooms and season with salt and pepper. Add the onion and sauté until the mushrooms are golden, 8 to 10 minutes.

2. Transfer the mixture to a large bowl and fold in $1^{1}/2$ cups of the salsa. Combine the remaining $1/2$ cup of salsa with the cilantro in a small bowl and set aside.

3. Heat a grill pan or large, heavy sauté pan over medium heat. Coat the pan lightly with nonstick cooking spray or add the 2 tablespoons of grapeseed oil and swirl to coat the pan.

4. To make the quesadillas, spread the bottom half of each tortilla with a $1/4$-inch-thick layer of the mushroom mixture. Top with 4 to 5 slices of the tofu, then fold the tortillas in half to make a half-moon shape. Carefully place the tortillas in the pan and brown, 4 to 5 minutes. With a large spatula, turn the tortillas and brown on the second side, 3 to 4 minutes. Transfer to a cutting board and cut into wedges. Serve with the extra salsa on the side.

BEVERAGE TIP
Grape type
Viognier

Characteristics
White peach, apricot,
spring flowers, white
pepper finish,
lush nectar

Recommendations
E. Guigal, Condrieu
Rhone Valley, France

Renwood
"Select Series"
California Cuvèe

TOMATO–KAFFIR LIME TURKEY "BOLOGNESE"

Unlike traditional Italian bolognese dishes, which require long simmering of ground meat and other ingredients to make a pasta sauce, this one's a breeze. I mean, *really* easy. Just sauté some ground turkey—which makes a deliciously light substitute for the usual meat—add the salsa, toss with pasta, and you're set.

As delicious as this is with spaghetti, you can also make a flavorful open-faced sandwich by spooning the turkey mixture onto crusty bread slices. Quick to prepare and satisfying to eat, this is *the* after-work dish.

Serves 4

1 pound spaghetti
2 tablespoons extra-virgin olive oil, plus additional, for serving
2 pounds ground turkey
Kosher salt and freshly ground black pepper to taste
2 cups Tomato–Kaffir Lime Salsa (page 98)
1/4 cup fresh basil leaves cut into 1/8-inch ribbons

1. In a large pot of boiling salted water, cook the pasta until TK; drain well and set aside.

2. Heat a large, heavy saucepan over high heat. Add the oil and swirl to coat the pan. Add the turkey and sauté, stirring, until it colors lightly, 5 to 6 minutes.

3. Season with salt and pepper. Add the salsa and basil and heat through, 4 to 5 minutes. Add the spaghetti and cook until it's heated through, about 2 minutes. Transfer to pasta bowls, drizzle a little additional oil over each portion, and serve.

MASTER RECIPE

TRY IT

Mix equal parts of the paste and mayonnaise for a sandwich spread or crudité dip.

For a deliciously spicy dumpling filling, blend 1/2 cup of paste per pound of ground pork. Or blend the paste with beef in the same proportions to make burgers.

Want a quick, warming soup? Mix 3/4 cup of the paste with 1 quart of good chicken stock and rice noodles.

GREEN CURRY PASTE

Curry pastes are some of the earliest convenience foods. They were created centuries ago to provide lots of flavor in a ready-to-use form: Just combine them with other aromatic ingredients, meat, vegetables, or fish, and there's your curry dish. In Thailand and other Southeast Asian countries the color of the paste often indicates the ingredients that dominate it; a green paste, like this one, is usually herb-based. My example uses basil, cilantro, and mint (for a bit of sweetness), so you know already how fragrant it is.

Yes, the paste calls for lots of ingredients, but the actual preparation goes quickly. And think of all the possibilities once you have it in the fridge.

Makes 4 cups
Lasts 2 weeks, refrigerated

5 dried Thai chiles or 5 fresh
  serrano chiles
2 tablespoons cumin seeds
5 tablespoons coriander seeds
2 tablespoons black peppercorns, plus
  freshly ground black pepper to taste
2 tablespoons kosher salt, plus
  additional for blanching
1 cup packed fresh cilantro leaves
  and stems
1 cup packed fresh basil leaves
1 cup packed fresh mint leaves

1 teaspoon ground turmeric
1/4 cup minced fresh galangal or ginger
1/3 cup minced garlic
3 lemongrass stalks,
  white parts only, minced
8 kaffir lime leaves, stemmed, or the
  grated zest of 2 limes
1/2 cup fresh lime juice
1/2 cup Thai fish sauce (nam pla)
1 cup medium shallots, sliced
2 cups Asian peanut oil or canola oil

1. In a small, heavy skillet combine the chiles, cumin seeds, coriander seeds, and peppercorns and heat over medium heat, stirring occasionally, just until the spices start to smoke, about 6 minutes. Using a spice grinder, grind the spices fine and set aside.

2. Meanwhile, fill a medium bowl with ice water. Bring a small saucepan of salted water to a boil, add the cilantro, basil, and mint, and blanch for 1 minute. Drain and transfer to the bowl of ice water. Drain, squeeze to remove as much water as possible, and set aside.

3. In a food processor, combine the turmeric, galangal, garlic, lemongrass, lime leaves, lime juice, and fish sauce and process to make a smooth purée. Add the shallots, reserved spices, the 2 tablespoons of salt, and the blanched herbs and purée again. With the machine running, drizzle in the oil to make a paste. Season with salt and pepper. Use or store.

BEVERAGE TIP
Grape type
Pinot Blanc

Characteristics
Off dry, crisp
honeydew/pear/apple
refreshing

Recommendations
Sipp Mack
Alsace, France

GREEN CURRY CHICKEN NOODLES

This one-wok dish features rice noodles. They were one of the first noodles I enjoyed and they remain my favorite today. I really love their mellow flavor, which makes a great contrast to the spicy green chile in this simple but delicious stir-fry.

Serves 4

1 pound boneless, skinless chicken thigh meat, cut into 1-inch dice
Kosher salt and freshly ground black pepper to taste
3 tablespoons grapeseed or canola oil
2 medium onions, thinly sliced
1 cup Green Curry Paste (page 106)
2 red bell peppers, cored, seeded, and cut into fine strips
1 pound rice noodles, soaked in hot water until soft, about 30 minutes, then drained
Juice of 3 limes plus 1 lime, quartered, for garnish

1. Season the chicken with salt and black pepper. Heat a wok or heavy sauté pan over high heat, add 2 tablespoons of the oil, and swirl to coat. Add the chicken and stir-fry until brown on all sides, then transfer to a bowl. (The chicken will continue cooking off the heat.)

2. Heat the wok over high heat. Add the remaining tablespoon of oil and swirl to coat the pan. Add the onions and stir-fry until soft, about 2 minutes. Add the curry paste and stir. Add the bell peppers, rice noodles, and chicken and heat through for about 5 minutes to ensure that the chicken is thoroughly cooked. Correct the seasoning with salt and pepper. Add the lime juice, stir, and garnish with the lime wedges. Serve immediately.

GRILLED GREEN CURRY–MARINATED SALMON AND EGGPLANT STEAKS

This grilled salmon and eggplant dish benefits from curry paste in a special way. Besides its intriguing flavor, the paste contains sufficient acid (in the form of the lime juice) to make it a great marinade for the fish—and for the eggplant, too.

  Maybe you've never thought of marinating vegetables before, but harder types, like eggplant and zucchini, can be enhanced this way.

Serves 4

1 large eggplant, stalk trimmed
Four 8-ounce salmon steaks, preferably center-cut, skin on
2 cups Green Curry Paste (page 106)
2 tablespoons grapeseed or canola oil, if needed
1 cup sour cream
Zest and juice of 2 limes
Steamed rice, for serving

1. Using a vegetable peeler, remove 1-inch strips of skin from the eggplant, leaving 2-inch strips of skin between the exposed flesh. Cut the eggplant into 1-inch rounds. Rub the salmon and eggplant on all sides with all but ¼ cup of the curry paste. Marinate, refrigerated, for 4 hours.

2. Prepare an outdoor grill, heat to hot, and spray the grill grid with nonstick cooking spray. Alternatively, heat a large grill pan or heavy skillet over high heat. Spray the grill pan with nonstick cooking spray or add the oil to the skillet and swirl to coat the pan. Grill or sauté the eggplant on one side until well colored, 6 to 8 minutes. Turn the eggplant and add the salmon to the grill. Grill until the eggplant is done on the second side, 6 to 8 minutes more, and the salmon is cooked, turning it once, 4 to 5 minutes per side for medium-rare.

3. Meanwhile, in a small bowl combine the remaining ¼ cup of curry paste, the sour cream, all but 1 teaspoon of the lime zest, and the lime juice, and mix. Mound the steamed rice on 4 serving plates. Top with the eggplant and salmon, dollop with the sour cream mixture, and sprinkle with the remaining zest. Serve.

BEVERAGE TIP
Beer

Characteristics
Crisp, light, clean

Recommendations
Foster's
Australia

GREEN CURRY CHICKEN BURGER

Burgers made with ground chicken or turkey tend to be a bit flavorless. This one is different, very different, due to the Green Curry Paste, which adds real zing. I like to serve this superior burger with Sweet Potato Fries (page 25) and slaw, preferably one made with Shallot-Soy Vinaigrette (page 116).

Serves 4

1 pound ground chicken
$1/2$ cup Green Curry Paste (page 106)
1 large very ripe tomato, sliced $1/4$-inch thick
Kosher salt and freshly ground black pepper, to taste
4 hamburger buns, toasted.

1. Prepare an outdoor grill and heat it to hot. In a large bowl combine the beef and curry paste and mix until just blended. Allow the meat to flavor, refrigerated, for at least 30 minutes and up to 2 hours.

2. Meanwhile, spread the tomato slices on a large plate and season them with the salt and pepper. Form 4 patties from the meat mixture about 1 inch thick.

3. Spray the grill grid with nonstick cooking spray and grill the burgers, turning once, until done, about 4 minutes per side for medium rare. Alternatively, heat a heavy grill pan or sauté pan, spray it with nonstick cooking spray, and grill the burgers. The burgers can also be broiled in a preheated broiler about 3 inches from the heat source. Make sure the burgers are cooked through by cutting into one and checking for doneness.

4. Place 2 tomato slices on each bun bottom, add the burgers and top with the remaining tomatoes. Finish with the bun tops and serve.

BEVERAGE TIP

Grape type
Grüner Veltliner

Characteristics
Off dry, grassy, lemon
tones, bit spicy

Recommendations
Fürsten Von
Liechtenstein
Wilfersdorf, Austria

SPICY GREEN CURRY ROCK SHRIMP "GUMBO"

After enjoying my first seafood gumbo (in New Orleans, naturally), I was surprised at how stick-to-your-ribs the dish is. With sausage, corn, and potatoes in it, it had every right to be. I soon became devoted to gumbos as a great meal-in-a-bowl dish.

This version follows in the hearty tradition. It uses rock shrimp—tiny specimens with a delicious lobsterlike taste—and, of course, the Green Curry Paste, so rather than the usual hot-sauce gumbo heat you get a wave of spicy flavors. Try it on a cool night with crusty bread.

MING'S TIPS

To dice the potatoes easily, first wash them, then, with a knife, square off all four "sides" including the tops and bottoms. Cut the potatoes along their length to make slices $1/2$ inch thick. Keep the slices together in a stack and slice the potato to make sticks about $1/2$ inch wide. Cut across the sticks to make $1/2$-inch cubes.

Serves 4

1 pound rock shrimp or regular small shrimp, peeled, veins removed, if
    necessary, rinsed, and drained
1 teaspoon sea salt, preferably Hawaiian pink
Juice of 1 lime
2 tablespoons grapeseed or canola oil
2 spicy pork sausages sliced $1/2$ inch thick
1 cup Green Curry Paste (page 106)
2 large potatoes, cut into $1/2$-inch dice
4 cups Master Chicken Broth (page 192) or low-sodium canned chicken broth
Kosher salt and freshly ground black pepper to taste
Kernels from 4 ears of corn
2 cups cored and shredded kale

1. In a small bowl, combine the shrimp with the sea salt and lime juice and set aside in the fridge.

2. Heat a small stockpot or Dutch oven over high heat. Add the oil and swirl to coat. Add the sausages and brown on all sides, 3 to 4 minutes. Stir in the curry paste and sauté for 1 minute. Add the potatoes and chicken broth and season with salt and pepper, keeping in mind that the shrimp have been seasoned with salt.

3. Bring to a simmer over medium heat and cook until the potatoes are tender and the liquid has reduced by about one quarter, 10 to 15 minutes. Add the shrimp, corn, and kale and cook until the shrimp are cooked through, 3 to 5 minutes more. Correct the seasoning with salt and pepper. Serve in heated pasta bowls.

To cut corn kernels from the cobs neatly and easily, slice off the large cob ends so each can stand straight without slipping. Place a small cutting board on a damp towel inside a large container like a deep rimmed sheet pan or dishwashing tub and cut the kernels off. They'll fall into the container rather than fly around.

IN THIS CHAPTER

DRESSINGS, DIPPING SAUCES, AND MARINADES

Vinaigrettes and other dressings aren't only for salads. When you think of them, as I do, as flavoring ingredients, you see their dish-making potential. To prepare Warm Shiitake and Corn Salad Frisée, for example, I add Shallot-Soy Vinaigrette to a mushroom and corn mixture, which flavors it deliciously while it cooks. Likewise, Five-Herb Vinaigrette and Sesame Tofu Caesar Dressing are used in dishes like Wok-Stirred Mushroom Salad Cups, a mushroom stir-fry served in crisp lettuce leaves.

The fundamental vinaigrette ingredients—oil and vinegar—are also the basis of marinades, which depend on an acid like vinegar to penetrate and flavor protein plus oil to carry flavor, as well as dipping sauces. Miso-Citrus Marinade, based on the traditional Japanese sake and miso pairing, adds bright-smoky taste to broiled salmon accompanied by pickled-plum-flavored rice and a simple but savory all-in-one dish of chicken roasted with vegetables. But you don't have to use marinades as an ingredient "soak" only. Soy-Dijon Marinade is added to the meat for the best hamburgers ever, and in Soy-Dijon Chicken Wings.

Dipping sauces are also vinaigrettes-by-another-name. (Or maybe it's vice versa.) Packed with herbs like basil and mint, and tangy with lime, Thai Lime Dipping Sauce can be used traditionally, as I do with our sensational Blue Ginger Crispy Calamari (it's also used to flavor the squid before it's fried), or as post-grilling flavor infusion for chicken plus dressing for accompanying noodles, spinach, and tomatoes in Thai Lime Chicken Salad. As you can see, the "vinaigrette" family is enormously versatile.

TRY IT
This works beautifully on everyday tossed greens and other impromptu salad combinations.

Like many vinaigrettes, the dressing doubles as a marinade for poultry, meat, and fish. For example, use it with peeled shrimp and scallops before grilling them.

For an intriguingly flavored cole slaw, marinate finely sliced red and/or white cabbage in the vinaigrette for 5 to 10 minutes.

SHALLOT-SOY VINAIGRETTE

This much-loved dressing is a Blue Ginger staple, on our menu since day one and probably there forever. It epitomizes the East-West culinary approach. Vinaigrette is, of course, *the* basic French salad dressing, a mixture of oil and vinegar to which mustard and sometimes shallots are added. For this Blue Ginger version, I use Chinese black and rice vinegars plus soy sauce, in addition to mustard and shallots, for cross-cultural flavor.

Makes 3½ cups
Lasts 2 weeks, refrigerated

1 cup grainy mustard
8 medium shallots, roughly chopped (about 1 cup)
¼ cup Chinese black vinegar, or balsamic vinegar
½ cup naturally brewed rice wine vinegar
¼ cup soy sauce
2 tablespoons sugar
2 cups grapeseed oil or canola oil
Kosher salt and freshly ground black pepper to taste

In a blender or food processor, combine the mustard, shallots, vinegars, soy sauce, and sugar and purée. With the machine running, slowly drizzle in the oil until an emulsion is formed. Season with salt and pepper, remembering that not much salt will be needed because of the soy sauce. Use or store.

BEVERAGE TIP
Grape type
Sauvignon Blanc

Characteristics
Bright citrus,
clean, herbacious

Recommendations
Cain Musque
Monterey, California

Cakebread Cellars
Napa Valley, California

WARM SHIITAKE AND CORN SALAD FRISÉE

When I cooked in France, I fell in love with a classic warm bistro salad made with frisée lettuce, sliced chicken gizzard, and *lardons* (bacon chunks), all topped with a poached egg. It was to die for—almost literally, because of its fat content. Here's my East–West version, which is every bit as satisfying as the bistro special, but much better for you. I use meaty shiitakes in place of the bacon and I add sweet corn, which contrasts beautifully with the Shallot-Soy Vinaigrette. Croutons made from crusty bread complete this delicious but simply made dish.

Serves 4

1 baguette sliced diagonally ¼ inch thick
2 tablespoons extra-virgin olive oil, plus additional for brushing on the
    baquette
2 cups fresh shiitake mushrooms sliced ¼ inch thick
Kernels from 3 ears of corn (see Ming's Tip, page 113)
4 scallions, white and green parts, thinly sliced
½ cup Shallot-Soy Vinaigrette (page 116)
2 heads of frisée lettuce, leaves separated, rinsed, dried, and torn, if large
Kosher salt and freshly ground black pepper to taste

1. Preheat the oven to 300°F. Place the baguette slices on a baking sheet, brush the slices with oil, and bake until golden, 10 to 12 minutes. Set aside.

2. Heat a wok or sauté pan over high heat. Add the 2 tablespoons of oil and swirl to coat the pan. Add the mushrooms and sauté until soft, 3 to 4 minutes. Add the corn and scallions and sauté until soft, about 2 minutes. Add the vinaigrette and heat thoroughly. (The vinaigrette will break.)

3. Place the frisée in a large bowl, pour the hot vinaigrette and vegetables over it, and toss well. Season with salt and pepper, toss, and serve with the baguette slices.

GRILLED ASIAN ANTIPASTO SALAD

Asian antipasto? Sure. My Asian ancestors served a kind of antipasto at their banquets that consisted of sliced cured meats (salami, anyone?), barbecued eel, and jellyfish, among other tidbits. My East–West version, which plays salty, buttery prosciutto against crunchy grilled radicchio, is really enticing. Tofu adds a creamy note without the richness that mozzarella, its Italian "counterpart," might.

Serves 4

2 whole red bell peppers
1/2 pound fresh shiitake mushrooms, stemmed
1 bunch of thin asparagus, ends removed
2 small heads of radicchio, cored and quartered lengthwise
1 package of firm tofu, sliced 1/2 inch thick
1 cup Shallot–Soy Vinaigrette (page 116)
Kosher salt and freshly ground black pepper to taste
1/2 pound very thinly sliced prosciutto, cut into 1/4-inch ribbons

1. Prepare an outdoor grill and heat to hot. Grill the peppers, turning, until well charred, about 15 minutes. Alternatively, grill the peppers under the broiler. Transfer the peppers to a bowl and cover it with plastic wrap. Allow the peppers to steam for 20 minutes, peel and seed them, then cut them into 1-inch strips.

2. Meanwhile, in a large bowl, combine the mushrooms, asparagus, radicchio, tofu, and 1/2 cup of the vinaigrette and toss gently to coat. Season with salt and pepper. Transfer to the grill and grill, turning as needed, until the vegetables have colored on all sides and are tender, 6 to 8 minutes. Alternatively, broil the ingredients about 6 inches from the heat source, turning as needed, 6 to 8 minutes. The asparagus will be done most quickly.

3. Lay the prosciutto on a large serving platter. Arrange the vegetables over it, drizzle with the remaining 1/2 cup of vinaigrette, and serve.

BEVERAGE TIP

Grape type
Gamay Noir

Characteristics
Layered cooked
cherries and
plums, chewy

Recommendations
Brick House
Willamette Valley,
Oregon

SHALLOT–SOY MARINATED CHICKEN BREAST WITH MELTED CABBAGE

Vinaigrettes can always double as marinades because their vinegar helps tenderize as well as flavor meats. This dish takes advantage of that fact to produce a deliciously moist roasted chicken breast. Actually, the part of the dish I love most is the melted cabbage. Growing up, I often ate cabbage steamed, braised, and stir-fried—methods that reduced the vegetable to luscious softness. In this recipe, cabbage is treated in just that way. I guess you could call the melted cabbage my version of mashed potatoes, as in the classic combo of chicken with mashed potatoes, which also inspired this dish.

Serves 4

4 large boneless chicken breasts with skin
1 cup Shallot-Soy Vinaigrette (page 116)
1 tablespoon grapeseed or canola oil
Kosher salt and freshly ground black pepper to taste
1/4 cup extra-virgin olive oil
1 bunch of scallions, white and green part separated and thinly sliced
1 large head of napa cabbage, cored and cut into 1/4-inch slices
Juice of 1 lemon plus the zest, minced

1. Preheat the oven to 400°F.

2. In a large bowl, combine the chicken and the vinaigrette and toss to coat the chicken. Cover and marinate, refrigerated, for at least 1 hour and up to 4 hours.

3. Heat a large, ovenproof sauté pan over high heat. Add the grapeseed oil and swirl to coat the pan. Season the chicken with salt and pepper, place in the pan skin side down, and sauté until brown, about 5 minutes. Turn the chicken and transfer, in the pan, to the oven. Roast until the chicken is cooked through, or until the juices run clear when the chicken is pricked with the tip of a knife in its thickest part, 12 to 15 minutes. Remove to a cutting board and allow to rest for 5 minutes, then cut the breast diagonally into 1/4-inch slices.

4. Meanwhile, in the same pan, heat the olive oil over high heat. Add the scallion whites and sauté until soft, 1 to 2 minutes. Add the cabbage, season with salt and pepper, and cook, stirring, until the cabbage is very soft, 5 to 6 minutes. Add the lemon juice and zest, stir, and correct the seasoning with salt and pepper.

5. Mound the cabbage in the center of a large serving plate. Surround with the chicken slices, garnish with the scallion greens, and serve.

FIVE-HERB VINAIGRETTE

I'm a big fan of "broken" vinaigrettes—those whose ingredients separate after the mixture stands for a while, like this one. I love seeing the way their parts come together again when shaken to become a tasty whole. Five-Herb Vinaigrette is intriguingly delicious and very versatile.

The recipe calls for dried herbs. You definitely want these, as opposed to fresh, as the dried ones won't darken over time. And here's a case where I really do recommend grapeseed oil, which contributes its own special nutty flavor.

Shake the vinaigrette when you're ready to use it.

Makes 3½ cups
Lasts 2 weeks, refrigerated

¼ cup Dijon mustard
¼ cup minced shallots
1 cup rice white vinegar
2 tablespoons Chinese black vinegar, or balsamic vinegar
2 tablespoons mirin
1 tablespoon sugar
2 tablespoons dried mint
2 tablespoons dried cilantro
2 tablespoons dried basil, preferably Thai
1 teaspoon dried thyme
2 tablespoons dried tarragon
2 cups grapeseed or canola oil

In a medium nonreactive bowl, combine the mustard, shallots, vinegars, mirin, sugar, mint, cilantro, basil, thyme, and tarragon. Whisk in the grapeseed oil. Use or store.

MARINATED TOMATO SALAD WITH SESAME-CRUSTED GOAT CHEESE

Almost everyone loves the classic Italian salad match of ripe tomatoes and sliced mozzarella. I've swapped sesame-crusted goat cheese for the mozzarella, which gives the dish a delicious Asian twist. The goat cheese is cut into rounds and sautéed to bring out the nutty flavor of the sesame seeds, but if you're feeling lazy, you can just toast the seeds and dip the cheese in them.

   Heirloom tomatoes are great for this, but you can use any ripe tomatoes, and any mixture of colors or sizes.

Serves 4

4 large ripe tomatoes, sliced ¼ inch thick
Sea salt
Freshly cracked black peppercorn
1 small onion, white or sweet (such as Vidalia, Maui, or Walla Walla), halved and
   very thinly sliced
Leaves from ½ bunch of basil, sliced into very thin ribbons
½ cup Five-Herb Vinaigrette (page 122)
1 cup all-purpose flour
3 eggs lightly beaten with 2 tablespoons water
½ cup sesame seeds
1 large log (8 to 12 ounces) of goat cheese, cut into twelve ½-inch slices
2 tablespoons extra-virgin olive oil

1. Arrange half of the tomatoes on 4 serving plates and season with the salt and pepper. Top with half the onions and half the basil, and drizzle with half the vinaigrette. Layer over the remaining tomatoes, season again, and top with the remaining onions and basil. Coat with the remaining vinaigrette. Set aside at room temperature for 1 hour.

2. Meanwhile, separately place the flour, egg and water mixture, and sesame seeds on 3 plates. Dip the cheese rounds into the flour and the egg mixture, then coat the flat surfaces of the rounds with the seeds. As you work, place the cheese disks on another plate. (These can be done in advance and stored in the fridge.)

3. Heat a large, nonstick sauté pan over medium heat. Add the oil and swirl to coat the pan. Add the goat cheese disks and sauté, turning once, until brown, 2 to 3 minutes per side.

4. Arrange the goat cheese on top of the tomato salads and serve immediately.

BEVERAGE TIP
Grape type
Arneis

Characteristics
Refreshing, pineapple-citrus, slight frizzante

Recommendations
Ceretto
Alba, Italy

MING'S TIP
To cut the cheese easily, use a thin-bladed knife warmed under hot water then dried.

WARM ROCK SHRIMP AND CELERY ROOT SALAD

When I worked at Fauchon, the fancy-food emporium in Paris, the staff was allowed to eat at a cafeteria supplied with food that hadn't sold. This wasn't a hardship; we enjoyed incredible dishes like truffled lobster in aspic and duck with exotic fruit. I, however, always made a beeline for the *céleri rémoulade*, a traditional pairing of crunchy celery root and a creamy sauce. I loved it, particularly dolloped onto crusty bread, with which I'd make my own "gourmet" sandwich. (Whenever I did this, the chef de cuisine would look at me with disdain—the polite word for it.)

This delicious warm salad owes its birth to my passion for celery root, which is as good heated as raw. Stir-fry with shrimp, tomatoes, and Five-Herb Vinaigrette, turn onto a plate, and there's your lovely dish.

Serves 4

$1/2$ pound mixed salad greens
2 tablespoons extra-virgin olive oil
1 pound rock shrimp, rinsed and dried, or peeled medium shrimp cut in thirds
Kosher salt and freshly ground black pepper to taste
$1/4$ cup thinly sliced scallions, white and green parts
2 medium celery roots, peeled and cut into $1/8$-inch matchsticks
$3/4$ cup Five-Herb Vinaigrette (page 122)
2 large tomatoes, cut into $1/4$-inch dice

1. Divide the greens among 4 plates.

2. Heat a wok or large sauté pan over high heat. Add the oil and swirl to coat. Add the shrimp, season with salt and pepper, and stir-fry until no longer raw-looking, about 1 minute. Add the scallions and celery root and stir-fry until just beginning to soften, 2 to 3 minutes. Add $1/2$ cup of the vinaigrette and toss. Remove from the heat, add the tomatoes, and correct the seasoning with salt and pepper.

3. Place mounds of the shrimp mixture on the greens. Drizzle the salad with the remaining $1/4$ cup of vinaigrette and serve.

GRILLED FIVE-HERB VEGETABLE PANZANELLA

I love bread salads, which combine the best of the starch and vegetable worlds. This version is particularly tasty, as you get an array of great veggies, including eggplant and fennel, plus crispy, vinaigrette-flavored croutons that give your choppers a nice workout.

Serves 4

1 small eggplant, ends trimmed, and cut lengthwise into $1/2$-inch-thick slices
1 large red onion, root and stem ends trimmed and cut into $1/4$-inch slices
1 large fennel, halved, cored, halved again, and cut lengthwise into $1/4$-inch-thick slices
2 red bell peppers, halved, seeded, and cut into $1/2$-inch slices
1 cup Five-Herb Vinaigrette (page 122)
Kosher salt and freshly ground black pepper, to taste
3 cups French or Italian bread cut into 1-inch cubes

1. Prepare an outdoor grill and heat to hot, or preheat the broiler.

2. In a large bowl, combine the eggplant, onion, fennel, peppers, and $3/4$ cup of the vinaigrette and toss to coat the vegetables evenly. Season with the salt and pepper.

3. Grill or broil the vegetables, turning often, until brown on all sides, 6 to 8 minutes. Transfer the vegetables to a cutting board, stacking them evenly, to finish cooking. Meanwhile, grill the bread, or toast it under the broiler, turning it often until evenly golden, about 5 minutes.

4. Chop the vegetables into 1-inch pieces. Just before serving, toss the croutons with the remaining vinaigrette, then toss the croutons with the vegetables. Correct the seasoning with the salt and pepper and serve from the bowl.

BEVERAGE TIP

Grape type
Dolcetto

Characteristics
Red cherry, cranberry,
medium acid, graceful

Recommendations
Pio Cesare
Alba, Italy

MING'S TIP

Middle, medium-size
leaves of the lettuce
make the best cups.
Shred the outer leaves
to make a bed for the
lettuce cups, if you like,
or use them for salads.

WOK-STIRRED MUSHROOM SALAD CUPS

I love dishes that contrast hot and cold, crisp and soft, as this one does. It's my takeoff on a Chinese favorite called *ma yee shaung shu* ("ants climbing a tree"), a delicious but time-consuming dish of minced squab, bamboo shoots, rice noodles, and lettuce. This much simplified version, great as an appetizer or hors d'oeuvre, features stir-fried mushrooms seasoned with Five-Herb Vinaigrette served in cool lettuce "cups." Every bite gives you hot, cold, soft, and crispy—in other words, pleasure.

Serves 4

2 heads of butter or Bibb lettuce, broken into cups
2 tablespoons extra-virgin olive oil
2 garlic cloves, sliced
$1/2$ pound fresh shiitake mushrooms, sliced $1/8$ inch thick
$1/2$ pound button mushrooms, sliced $1/8$ inch thick
$1/2$ pound oyster mushrooms, torn into bite-size pieces
$1/2$ cup Five-Herb Vinaigrette (page 122), plus additional if desired
Kosher salt and freshly ground black pepper to taste

1. Arrange the lettuce on 4 serving plates.

2. Heat a wok or heavy sauté pan over high heat. Add the oil and swirl to coat the pan. Add the garlic and stir-fry until light tan, about 30 seconds. Add the shiitake and button mushrooms and stir-fry for 1 to 2 minutes. Add the oyster mushrooms and stir-fry for 1 minute more. Add the vinaigrette and toss. Season with salt and pepper.

3. Fill the lettuce cups with the mushroom mixture. Drizzle with additional vinaigrette, if you like, and serve immediately.

MASTER RECIPE

TRY IT
Use the dressing with shredded cabbage for a special cole slaw.

Great for binding a potato salad.

Makes a delicious sandwich spread.

MING'S TIP
To save work, buy ready-peeled garlic cloves.

SESAME TOFU CAESAR DRESSING

I've always loved Caesar salad. Before I'd ever made the dish, though, I assumed its creamy dressing actually used cream. Wrong! Its silky texture results from emulsification with raw egg. This delicious version avoids that ingredient (which can pose health risks) and, for smoothest texture, uses tofu instead. Garlic, a key element of the original, stays, but is cooked first for less bite and a rounder, sweeter flavor. If you don't like anchovies, a traditional Caesar ingredient, just up the olive quotient. You'll still have a great dressing.

Makes 3 cups
Lasts 2 weeks, refrigerated

2 cups plus 2 tablespoons extra-virgin olive oil
16 large garlic cloves (about 2 heads)
Kosher salt and freshly ground black pepper to taste
4 anchovy fillets
6 Niçoise or other black olives, pitted
⅓ cup Dijon mustard
6 ounces silken tofu, drained
Juice of 2 lemons
1 tablespoon Asian sesame oil

1. Heat a sauté pan over medium heat. Add the 2 tablespoons of oil and swirl to coat the pan. Add the garlic, season with salt and pepper, and sauté until the garlic is lightly brown, 2 to 3 minutes.

2. In a food processor combine the garlic, anchovy fillets, olives, and mustard and purée until smooth. Add the tofu and lemon juice and purée. With the machine running, drizzle in the remaining 2 cups of olive oil and the sesame oil. Correct the seasoning with salt and pepper. Use or store.

BEVERAGE TIP

Grape type
Albariño

Characteristics
Fresh, spritzy,
lime-apple

Recommendations
Quinta da Aveleda
Penafiel, Portugal

ASIAN CHICKEN SALAD WITH BABY HEARTS OF ROMAINE

Food fads are funny. Caesar salad was devised about 80 years ago and has, since then, been in and out of fashion. Right now it's really in. Why not make a delicious Caesar salad of my own? Here it is, perfect for a light supper or easy first course.

Serves 4

2 tablespoons grapeseed or canola oil, if needed
4 boneless, skinless chicken breasts
2 thick slices of sourdough or other crusty bread
2 tablespoons extra-virgin olive oil
4 baby hearts of romaine, cored and leaves separated
1$\frac{1}{2}$ cups Sesame Tofu Caesar Dressing (page 130), plus additional, if desired
Kosher salt and freshly ground black pepper to taste, plus freshly cracked black
  peppercorns, for garnish
$\frac{1}{2}$ tablespoon toasted white sesame seeds (see Ming's tip, page 239)
$\frac{1}{2}$ tablespoon toasted black sesame seeds (see Ming's tip, page 239)

1. Preheat the oven to 350°F.

2. Heat an outdoor grill to hot. Alternatively, heat a grill pan or large heavy sauté pan over high heat, add the grapeseed oil, and swirl to coat the pan. Grill or sauté the chicken breasts until just cooked through, turning once, about 4 minutes per side. Cut the breasts diagonally into long slices $\frac{1}{4}$ inch thick.

3. Cut the bread into 1-inch cubes. In a medium bowl, toss the cubes with the olive oil. Transfer the bread to a baking tray and toast in the oven until golden brown, 8 to 10 minutes. Cool.

4. In a large salad bowl, toss the chicken with the romaine, dressing, and croutons. (Make sure the romaine is well coated.) Season with salt and freshly ground black pepper.

5. Arrange the salad on 4 serving plates so the chicken rests on the lettuce. Garnish with the sesame seeds and cracked black peppercorns, drizzle with additional dressing if you like, and serve.

BEVERAGE TIP
Grape type
Chardonnay, Pinot Noir,
Pinot Meunier

Characteristics
Toasty, citrusy,
green plum

Recommendations
Veuve Clicquot Brut NV
Reims, France

MING'S TIP
I suggest a cottage or
ruffle cut for the potatoes
(they will have ridges
throughout their surfaces).
You can achieve this with
a mandoline or other
specialty slicer. Otherwise,
plain slicing is fine.

CRUSTED COD AND ZUCCHINI WITH CHIPS AND CAESAR DIPPING SAUCE

Here's my version of fish and chips. The best rendition of that combo I've ever had was served in New Zealand, where the fish was incredibly fresh and the breading super-light. I've tried to follow that principle here, using panko (fine Japanese bread crumbs), which coat the fish delicately. With fried zucchini and a Caesar-dressing dip added to the mix, this version's a feast.

I recommend an electric fryer for this and similar dishes; they're safe, relatively mess-free, and easy to use. Next best is a small stockpot filled one-third full with oil; a tall-sided pot minimizes the possibility of splatter, so frying's neater.

Serves 4

Canola oil, for frying
3 large russet potatoes, washed and cottage-cut (see Ming's Tip, left), or sliced 1/4 inch thick
1 cup all-purpose flour
4 eggs, lightly beaten
2 cups panko (Japanese bread crumbs) or regular unflavored bread crumbs
2 pounds skinless cod fillet, cut diagonally into 1-inch-thick slices
1 large zucchini, cut diagonally into long 1/4-inch-thick rounds
Kosher salt and freshly ground black pepper to taste
1 cup Sesame Tofu Caesar Dressing (page 130)

1. Fill an electric fryer with the oil to the designated mark, or fill a small stockpot one-third full. Heat the oil to 350°F. Add the potatoes, in batches if necessary, and cook until lightly colored, 3 to 5 minutes. Remove, drain them on paper towels, and set aside.

2. Place the flour, eggs, and panko separately in 3 shallow dishes. Dredge the cod and zucchini in the flour, eggs, and then the panko. Make certain the oil has returned to 350°F., then fry the cod and zucchini in the hot oil until brown, 4 to 6 minutes for the cod and 3 to 5 minutes for the zucchini. Remove and drain both on paper towels. Season with salt and pepper.

3. Reheat the oil to 350°F. Return the reserved potatoes, and fry them until golden, 2 to 3 minutes. Remove, drain on paper towels, and season with salt and pepper.

4. Place the dressing in a ramekin. Line a large decorative bowl with parchment paper or paper towels and pile the fish, chips, and zucchini into it. Serve with the dressing for dipping.

MASTER RECIPE

TRY IT

Add grapeseed oil to the
sauce in the proportion of
2 oil to 1 sauce. You'll have
a great vinaigrette that's
perfect for seafood and
celery-root salads.

Use the sauce for "ceviche
cooking" cod, salmon,
and shrimp.

Marinate chicken legs
and thighs in the sauce,
then fry.

MING'S TIP

It's perfectly all right to
use bottled lime juice for
this, as long as it's real
juice. (Check juice labels.)
Fresh or bottled, lime
juice sometimes has a
bitter-tasting "edge." Taste
the juice you're going to
use, and if necessary, add
up to a tablespoon of
sugar to balance it.

THAI LIME DIPPING SAUCE

This dipping sauce, fresh with herbs and tangy with lime, is Blue Ginger's most
requested recipe. It's particularly awesome with our crispy calamari (see page 140)
as well as with spring rolls, dumplings, and similar bites. It's based on the traditional Thai dip called *cha-gio,* which gets its savor from fish sauce. That salty
ingredient is nicely balanced with lime juice.

The herbs darken as the sauce ages; this isn't a taste problem (quite the opposite, as the flavor deepens over time) but the sauce *will* loose its looks. If this
bothers you, make and store the sauce "base" only, then chop and add herbs an
hour before serving it. Or strain out any tired herbs from "old" sauce and replace
them with fresh.

Makes about 5 cups
Lasts 1 week, refrigerated

2 cups Thai fish sauce (nam pla)
3 cups fresh or bottled lime juice
1/2 cup chopped fresh cilantro
1/2 cup chopped fresh basil
1/2 cup chopped fresh mint
1 tablespoon peeled and minced fresh ginger

In a large nonreactive bowl, combine the ingredients and mix. Use or store.

BEVERAGE TIP
Grape type
Sauvignon Blanc

Characteristics
Crisp, mango,
passion fruit

Recommendations
Brancott
Marlborough,
New Zealand

Villa Maria,
Marlborough,
New Zealand

MING'S TIP
Pink peppercorns are
not true peppercorns,
but a dried roseplant
berry. Their flavor—
pungent, with a slight
sweetness—can be very
appealing. Available
freeze-dried or in brine
or water.

SCALLOP AND MANGO CEVICHE

Ceviche is food "cooked" without heat. I fell in love with the technique, which uses citric acid or vinegar to firm and therefore "cook" protein, when I traveled to Corsica and other Mediterranean spots. For me, ceviches always speak of summer. Here, mango adds its exotic sweetness to scallops, which cook in the flavorful dipping sauce.

As with all ceviches, freshness is key. Make sure your scallops are pristine enough to eat raw.

Serves 4

8 large sea scallops, sliced into ¼-inch disks
1 cup Thai Lime Dipping Sauce (page 136)
¼ pound mâche, mesclun, or other mixed small greens
1 large shallot, thinly sliced
1 mango, flesh removed from the pit and sliced lengthwise ⅛ inch thick
Juice of 2 limes
1 teaspoon pink peppercorns or cracked black pepper to taste

1. In a nonreactive bowl, combine the scallops with the Thai Lime Dipping Sauce and toss. Marinate, refrigerated, for 10 minutes.

2. Arrange a layer of the mâche on chilled plates. Top each portion with 3 scallop slices, half the shallot, and all of the mango. Top with the remaining scallop slices and shallot. Pour over the lime juice. Sprinkle with the peppercorns, crushing them with your fingers as you do so. Serve immediately.

BEVERAGE TIP

Grape type

Chardonnay

Characteristics

Racy, crisp, yuzu-citrus

Recommendations

Perrier-Jouet

Epernay, France

Schramsberg

Napa Valley,

California

MING'S TIPS

The recipe calls for all-purpose flour and sweet-potato flour. The latter, which is available in Asian markets, adds a slight sweetness to the crust and helps ensure crispness. You can, however, substitute cornstarch.

BLUE GINGER CRISPY CALAMARI

Fried calamari with a dipping sauce is one of America's most popular starters. That's understandable: Pair crispy squid with a tantalizing sauce and you've got great eating. This spice-fragrant version is superior in every way. A preliminary marination helps ensure tender squid, as does quick frying.

You can grind toasted whole spices or toast them already ground. Fresh and frozen squid work equally well here, but if you buy fresh, you get to ask your fish seller to clean the squid for you. (And make sure he gives you the tentacles—the best part!) I recommend flat strainers for moving the squid from its marinating bath to the coating mixture, and to help with the coating; they're a small investment with a big convenience payoff (or use regular large strainers). In any case, you'll love the dish as much as our Blue Ginger diners do.

Whenever I teach this dish to cooks, I make sure they understand the importance of listening as the squid cooks. As soon as the oil's bubbling sound dies away the squid is done.

Serves 4

1 teaspoon ground cumin
1 teaspoon ground coriander
1 teaspoon ground fennel
1 teaspoon ground white peppercorn
1 tablespoon kosher salt
Canola oil, for frying
2 cups Thai Lime Dipping Sauce (page 136), plus $1/2$ cup, for dipping
2 cups all-purpose flour
2 cups sweet-potato flour or cornstarch
2 pounds calamari, cleaned and cut into $1/2$-inch rings
2 tablespoons thinly sliced scallions, white and green parts

1. In a small frying pan, combine the cumin, coriander, fennel, and white peppercorns. Toast over medium heat, stirring, until just smoking, 4 to 5 minutes. Cool and transfer to a small serving bowl or ramekin. Add the salt and mix. Set aside.

2. Fill an electric fryer with the oil to the designated mark, or fill a small stockpot one-third full. Heat the oil to 375°F.

RECIPE CONTINUES

3. Place a flat strainer in a large bowl into which it just fits and fill the bowl with the Thai Lime Dipping Sauce. In another large bowl, combine the flours.

4. Working in batches, place the calamari in the first bowl and marinate for 10 seconds only. Using the strainer, lift the calamari from the bowl and transfer it to the bowl with the flours. With a second flat strainer, dip and lift the calamari in the flours, coating it so no moisture is detectable. Shake the squid in the strainer to remove all excess coating.

5. Transfer the squid to the oil and fry only until the bubbling sound dies away, 30 to 45 seconds. (The calamari will have colored to a golden brown.) Using a flat strainer, transfer the squid to paper towels to drain. Season the squid with the flavored salt, garnish with the scallions, and serve immediately with the dipping sauce.

VARIATION

To make a fabulous crispy calamari hoagie, smear a split submarine roll generously with Korean Tartar Sauce (see Ming's Tip, page 82) or homemade or store-bought tartar sauce, then add chopped Romaine lettuce leaves, or your favorite salad greens. Drizzle with Thai Lime Dipping Sauce (page 136) or fresh lime juice, top with freshly cooked crispy calamari, add some more lettuce, and top with the remaining bread.

BEVERAGE TIP

Grape type
Sauvignon Blanc

Characteristics
Fresh, clean, pineapple

Recommendations
"Pur Sang" Pouilly-Fumè
Didier Dageneau,
Loire Valley, France

THAI LIME CHICKEN SALAD

If you've ever tried a summer roll, you know they usually contain a protein like shrimp, rice or mung beans, lettuce, basil, and lime juice, all wrapped in rice paper. This deconstructed version is all filling, made with grilled chicken breast, spinach, rice noodles, and, of course, the Thai Lime Dipping Sauce. I love this salad because it contrasts warm chicken with cool ingredients, but you can make the chicken in advance, if you like, and serve it cool, too.

Serves 4

2 tablespoons grapeseed or canola oil, if needed
8 ounces rice noodles
4 boneless, skinless chicken breasts
Kosher salt and freshly ground black pepper to taste
1/2 cup Thai Lime Dipping Sauce (page 136)
1/4 cup canola oil
1/2 pound baby spinach leaves
1 pint cherry tomatoes, halved

1. Prepare an outdoor grill and heat to hot. Spray the grid well with nonstick cooking spray. Alternatively, heat a grill pan or large heavy sauté pan over high heat. Add the grapeseed oil and swirl to coat the pan.

2. Combine the noodles with hot tap water to cover and allow to soak until soft, about 30 minutes. Drain well.

3. Meanwhile, lightly season the chicken with salt and pepper. Grill or sauté the chicken on both sides until colored and the juices run clear when the breasts are pierced with the tip of a knife, 8 to 10 minutes total. Allow the breasts to cool until warm.

4. Slice the breasts 1/2 inch thick. In a bowl large enough to hold it, combine the chicken with 1/4 cup of the Thai Lime Dipping Sauce and marinate for 10 minutes.

5. Meanwhile, place the remaining 1/4 cup of sauce in a large mixing bowl and whisk in the canola oil. Correct the seasoning with salt and pepper. Add the noodles, spinach, and tomatoes and toss. Add the chicken, including the marinade, and toss well. Serve immediately in large chilled bowls.

MASTER RECIPE

TRY IT

Marinades provide foun-
dation flavors for many
dishes. Miso Citrus Marinade is particularly good
with fatty fish like black
cod, salmon, or butterfish,
whose flesh can stand up
to its ingredients (as
opposed to leaner fish that
tend to dry out in acid or
salty marinades). You can
also use the marinade
with shrimp and scallops.

Great as a crudité dip.

Use the marinade to glaze
grilled or broiled tofu.

MISO-CITRUS MARINADE

This recipe is based on a traditional Japanese marinade that pairs sake and miso.
I've brightened the classic blend by adding ponzu, the Japanese dipping sauce
made with citrus juice, among other flavorful ingredients. Both sake and ponzu
help "cook" the marinade into animal and fish protein, which is why the marinade
delivers such deep flavor.

Make sure to buy ponzu without added soy sauce.

Makes 5½ cups
Lasts 2 weeks, refrigerated

1 cup sake
1 cup ponzu
½ cup sugar
2 cups light miso (shiro-miso)
3 tablespoons peeled and minced fresh ginger
1 cup grapeseed or canola oil

In a large bowl, combine the sake, ponzu, and sugar and whisk until the sugar is
dissolved. Whisk in the miso until smooth. Add the ginger, then whisk in the oil
gradually, to emulsify the mixture. Store in the refrigerator.

BROILED MISO-CITRUS SALMON WITH UMEBOSHI RICE

This dish of simply broiled marinated salmon, accompanied by rice flavored with Japanese pickled plums (umeboshi), is super-tasty. The tart-salty umeboshi (you can substitute capers, if you like) make a perfect foil for the salmon's richness. Besides adding great flavor, the marinade helps give the fish a tempting crust.

Serves 4

4 salmon fillets (5 to 8 ounces each), preferably center-cut, skin on
2 cups Miso-Citrus Marinade (page 144)
Freshly ground black pepper to taste
4 cups steamed sushi rice (see Ming's Tip, right)
6 umeboshi (Japanese pickled plums), pitted and chopped, or 2 teaspoons
   drained capers
2 tablespoons thinly sliced scallion greens

1. In a large bowl, combine the salmon and the marinade and marinate, refrigerated, for 4 hours.

2. If your broiler is in the oven, place a rack in the center of the oven. Place a heavy baking sheet or broiling tray on the rack (or place the broiling tray in the broiling compartment), and turn the temperature control to broil. When the tray is very hot, remove it and spray it with nonstick cooking spray (do not turn off the broiler). Remove the salmon from the marinade and pat dry. Lightly season the salmon with the pepper, then place it skin side up on the tray. Broil the salmon until medium rare, 6 to 8 minutes, or to the degree of doneness you prefer. (Be careful not to burn the skin; if the skin looks like it's charring before the flesh is cooked, lower the sheet tray.)

3. Meanwhile, in a medium bowl, combine the rice, umeboshi, and scallions and mix. Dampen a rice bowl or other small bowl and fill with one quarter of the rice mixture. Unmold the rice onto a dinner plate and top with a salmon fillet. Repeat with the remaining rice and fish fillets.

BEVERAGE TIP
Grape type
Chardonnay,
Pinot Noir,
Pinot Meunier

Characteristics
Cranberry, cherry,
ripe tomatoes, zesty

Recommendations
Schramsberg Brut Rosé
Anderson Valley,
California

MING'S TIP
Before cooking sushi rice, place it in a bowl and add water to cover generously. Swish the rice to rinse off residual starch, pour off the water, and repeat until the water runs clear. Place the rice in a saucepan with a tight-fitting lid, flatten the rice with your palm, and, without removing your hand, add water until it just touches the highest knuckle on your hand. Cover the pan and bring to a boil over high heat, reduce the heat to medium and simmer until the rice absorbs all the water, about 30 minutes. Turn off the heat and let the rice stand, covered, for about 20 minutes to plump the grains.

GRILLED MISO-CITRUS SCALLOP LOLLIPOPS

Coming up with a great hors d'oeuvre can be a challenge. You need something delicious that can also be picked up and enjoyed without mess. These scallop lollipops—so called because the skewered portobello-wrapped scallops resembles the candy—are just the thing.

The idea for these came after a visit to the Minnesota State Fair, where I first saw mac and cheese on a stick (skewered chunks of the casserole breaded and fried), among other brochette innovations. A little East–West refinement of traditional bacon-wrapped scallops (the portobellos replace the meat) resulted in these bites, which also make a fine starter when served atop some dressed greens.

Soak the wooden skewers in cold water for 1 hour before grilling.

Makes 15 pieces; serves 3 to 5 as a first course

2 large portobello mushrooms, stemmed
1 pound medium sea scallops
2 cups Miso-Citrus Marinade (page 144)
2 tablespoons grapeseed or canola oil, plus ¼ cup more, if needed
Kosher salt and freshly ground black pepper to taste

IF SERVING AS A FIRST COURSE
¼ pound mixed greens
1 lemon

15 to 20 5-inch wooden skewers, soaked in cold water for 1 hour

1. With a spoon scrape the gills from the mushroom caps. Set aside the caps.

2. Toss the scallops with the marinade in a medium bowl. Marinate in the refrigerator for 2 to 3 hours.

3. Prepare a grill, heat to hot, and spray the grid with nonstick cooking spray. Alternatively, heat a grill pan or large sauté pan over high heat.

RECIPE CONTINUES

4. Lightly rub the portobellos with 2 tablespoons of the oil and season with salt and pepper. If using a pan, add 2 additional tablespoons of oil and swirl to coat the pan. Grill or sauté the mushrooms, turning once, until brown, 8 to 10 minutes total. Transfer the mushrooms to a medium bowl and cover with plastic wrap so the mushrooms can steam to complete their cooking, about 15 minutes. Cut the mushrooms into ¼-inch-thick slices.

5. Remove the scallops from the marinade and wipe to remove excess marinade. Encircle each scallop with 1 or 2 portobello slices then insert a skewer through the center to make a "handle" and hold the mushroom in place. Place 2 scallops on each skewer. If using a pan, reheat over high heat, add the remaining 2 tablespoons of oil, and swirl to coat the pan. Lightly pepper the scallops and, working in batches, if using a pan, sauté the lollipops, turning once, until the scallops are cooked, about 3 minutes per side. If using a grill, grill until the scallops are cooked through, turning once, about 2 minutes on each side.

6. If serving as an hors d'oeuvre, arrange the lollipops on an oval platter. To serve as a starter, divide the greens among 4 plates. Top with the lollipops, squeeze the juice from the lemon over the lollipops, and serve.

ROASTED MISO-CITRUS CHICKEN

My first great roast chicken in Paris came from a neighborhood "deli," where I smelled the chicken turning on a rotisserie before I saw it. When I tracked that amazing smell to its source, I devoured its crackling skin and supremely flavorful meat on the spot.

I've dreamed of "reproducing" that bird, and this recipe is a giant step in that direction. The Miso-Citrus Marinade adds flavor to the chicken, but also enhances its natural taste. Cooked with potatoes and other vegetables, this makes a one-pot feast.

Serves 3 or 4

One 5- to 7-pound chicken, preferably organic and/or free-range or kosher, washed and dried
2 cups Miso-Citrus Marinade (page 144)
3 large baking potatoes, washed and sliced $1/2$ inch thick
1 large yellow onion, sliced $1/8$ inch thick
One 1-pound bag peeled baby carrots
2 tablespoons extra-virgin olive oil
2 lemons, halved
Kosher salt and freshly ground black pepper to taste

1. Place the chicken on a plate. Rub the chicken inside and out with the marinade and marinate, refrigerated, for at least 4 hours and preferably overnight.

2. Place a heavy baking sheet or large ovenproof skillet in the oven and preheat the oven to 525°F.

3. Meanwhile, in a large bowl, combine the potatoes, onions, carrots, oil and the juice of the lemons. (Stuff the lemon halves inside the chicken's cavity.) Season the vegetables with the salt and pepper..

4. Pull out the oven rack with the tray and spray with nonstick cooking spray. Turn the vegetables onto the tray (be careful, there will be a lot of sizzling). Place the chicken on the vegetables breast side up, and roast until the chicken is evenly brown, 25 to 30 minutes. (You may need to rotate the chicken to ensure this.) Tent the chicken with foil, reduce the oven to 325°F., and continue to roast until the juices run clear when a leg joint is pricked with a paring knife, 25 to 30 minutes more. Halfway through the cooking period, lift the chicken and turn the vegetables.

5. Transfer the chicken to a cutting board and allow it to rest for 10 minutes. Using a spatula, carefully scrape the vegetables from the pan and place them on a large platter. Place the chicken on top of the vegetables and carve it at table, or carve the chicken, place the pieces on top of the vegetables, and serve.

BEVERAGE TIP

Grape type
Pinot Noir

Characteristics
Spicy black cherry,
light cedar

Recommendations
Flowers
Sonoma Coast,
California

MING'S TIP

To tell if the chicken is done, poke the point of a paring knife into a leg joint and wait 5 seconds. Carefully touch to lower lip. If the knife is hot, the chicken is cooked.

MASTER RECIPE

This is great for marinating "steak" fish like salmon and swordfish. Marinate the fish for 1 hour before cooking it.

Brush the marinade on roasted vegetables such as corn or portobellos.

Great for marinating chicken, pork chops, or steak before grilling or broiling.

MING'S TIP
A mortar and pestle is the easiest and most efficient tool for crushing peppercorns. But you can also crush them by placing a heavy pan over the peppercorns and pressing down on it with all your weight.

SOY-DIJON MARINADE

This is my "classic" marinade. It combines Dijon mustard—the best mustard, in my opinion—with soy sauce, wine, and herbs to produce a truly enhancing blend. I mean, this marinade *really* does the job, and not only for meat and poultry, but also for thick-fleshed mushrooms like portobellos or creminis.

Makes 6 cups
Lasts 2 weeks, refrigerated

1/4 cup cracked black peppercorns, plus freshly ground black pepper to taste
Kosher salt to taste
1 cup red wine
1 1/2 cups Dijon mustard
1/2 cup naturally brewed soy sauce
8 sprigs of fresh thyme, chopped, or 2 tablespoons dried
1/2 cup minced garlic
2 1/2 cups canola oil

In a small, dry sauté pan, heat the peppercorns over medium-high heat, stirring, until the peppercorns are fragrant and just begin to smoke, 2 to 4 minutes. Transfer to a medium nonreactive bowl and add the salt, wine, mustard, soy sauce, thyme, and garlic. Whisk in the canola oil gradually to emulsify the mixture. Use or store.

BEVERAGE TIP

Grape type
Cabernet Sauvignon
blend

Characteristics
Ripe plums,
extracted black berries,
light tobacco

Recommendations
Cain Five
Napa Valley, California

MING'S TIP

American lamb (espe-
cially Niman Ranch) is
tops. At Blue Ginger we
also serve New Zealand
lamb, which yields
smaller chops and has a
milder taste. You might
want to try it, if it's in
your market.

ROASTED SOY-DIJON LAMB RACKS WITH SMASHED BLUE CHEESE–SPINACH POTATOES

There's nothing like rack of lamb for simple yet luxurious eating. This version bows to traditional rack recipes in its use of thyme and mustard (here, they're in the marinade), but uses a hot skillet for an initial, flavor-building sear.

The accompaniments are also special. We served the chops with blue-cheese whipped potatoes at the restaurant and couldn't make enough of that side. (If you're not a blue-cheese fan, you can use Cheddar instead.) In this version, the cheese-flavored potatoes are smashed with a potato masher for a great rough texture. Wilted spinach, flavored with the lamb's juices, completes the dish.

Serves 4

2 large lamb racks, fat cap removed (have the butcher do this for you)
2 cups Soy-Dijon Marinade (page 152)
4 large baking potatoes, washed
1 cup heavy cream
1 cup crumbled blue cheese, such as Roquefort, Gorgonzola, Saga Blue, or
   Cabot Blue
Kosher salt and freshly ground black pepper to taste
1/2 pound baby spinach

1. Place the lamb racks in a baking dish and rub them with the marinade. Marinate the racks, covered with foil and refrigerated for 8 hours or overnight. Turn the racks during marination to ensure even flavoring.

2. Preheat the oven to 400°F. Wrap each potato in foil and prick several times with a fork through the foil. Bake the potatoes until soft, about 45 minutes. Remove the potatoes, turn the oven up to 525°F., and place a large, heavy skillet or ovenproof sauté pan in the oven to heat.

RECIPE CONTINUES

3. Meanwhile, in a large saucepan heat the cream over high heat until it comes to a simmer. Reduce the heat to medium and simmer until the cream is reduced by half, about 10 minutes. Add the cheese and stir to blend.

4. Place the hot potatoes in a large bowl and use a potato masher or 2 large forks to smash them, skin and all. Fold the hot cream mixture into the potatoes and season with salt and pepper. Return the potatoes to the saucepan, and cover to keep hot.

5. Place the lamb racks in the heated pan fat side down (they will sizzle). Roast the racks, allowing the pan heat to color them, for about 5 minutes. Turn the racks right side up and continue to roast them until cooked, 5 to 8 minutes for medium-rare.

6. Place the spinach on a large plate. Top with the racks and allow the spinach to soften from the racks' heat, about 10 minutes. (The juice from the racks will collect on the spinach.) Transfer the spinach and its juice to the saucepan with the potatoes and mix.

7. Mound the potato mixture in the center of 4 serving plates. Slice each rack into 8 double chops and place 2 on top of each potato portion. Serve.

BEVERAGE TIP

Grape type
Petite Syrah

Characteristics
Chocolate, raspberry,
blackberry

Recommendations
Guenoc
North Coast, California

MING'S TIP

Everyone seems to prefer one type of ground beef to another for burgers. At the restaurant we grind hanger steak for our burgers, but ground chuck and sirloin make great burgers, too. Just remember that if the meat you use is too lean your burgers will be dry and lack flavor.

PAN-SEARED SOY-DIJON HAMBURGER ON TOAST

I've never met a hamburger I didn't like. (Well, almost never.) Prepared well, this quintessential American food satisfies everyone. To make it even more of a good thing, I add Soy–Dijon Marinade to the meat before cooking it, and I serve the burgers on toast, as opposed to a bun, so you get just the right ratio of bread to meat. (I thank Louis' Lunch of New Haven, Connecticut, for the idea.) Served with tomato, lettuce, and red onion, this is a super burger, especially when accompanied by pickles and chips.

Serves 4

2 pounds ground beef
1/2 cup Soy-Dijon Marinade (page 152)
Kosher salt and freshly ground
 black pepper to taste
2 tablespoons unsalted butter

8 slices of bread, toasted
8 tender inner leaves of romaine
 lettuce, shredded
1 large tomato, sliced 1/4 inch thick
1 large red onion, sliced 1/4 inch thick

1. In a large, chilled bowl, combine the meat and marinade and, using your hands, mix gently just until the marinade is incorporated. Do not overwork the mixture. Form 4 patties, each the size of the bread slices. Lightly season the patties with salt and pepper.

2. Heat a large, nonstick sauté pan over high heat. Add the butter and when it melts, swirl to coat the pan. Sauté the burgers, turning once, until done, 2 to 4 minutes per side for medium-rare.

3. Place a slice of toast on each of 4 serving plates. Cover with the romaine and top with the burgers, tomato, and onion. Top with the remaining toast to make sandwiches, slice each diagonally, and serve.

BEVERAGE TIP

Beer

Characteristics

Bright, clean, refreshing

Recommendations

Sam Adams

Summer Ale

Boston, Massachusetts

Paulaner Heffewiesen,

Germany

Serve with lemon

MING'S TIP

Mom's tip, actually. She taught me that you can refresh oil that's been used for frying by frying a few cabbage leaves in it.

SOY-DIJON CHICKEN WINGS

I have it on paper: In 1989 at Cornell University I consumed 115 chicken wings in an hour. (This is not on my résumé, however.) That should give you some idea of my commitment to those addictive morsels, especially when prepared "Buffalo" style. This dish is the result of wanting to take those much-loved wings in a different direction.

As with the original, these wings are deep-fried for crispness and served with chilled celery sticks. But instead of the accompanying blue-cheese dip, I bathe the cooked wings in Soy–Dijon Marinade with added cheese for an awesome finish. These work equally well for munching or for supper, for few or a crowd.

Serves 3 or 4

1 small head of celery, stem end removed, washed
Canola oil, for frying
2 pounds chicken wings, separated into drumettes and wings (discard the tips)
1 cup crumbled blue cheese
1 cup Soy-Dijon Marinade (page 152)

1. Fill a medium bowl with water and add ice. Separate the celery head into stalks, trim the ends and leaves, and cut into 4-inch lengths, halving any wide sticks. Add to the bowl and set aside.

2. Fill an electric fryer with oil to the designated mark and heat to 375°F. Alternatively, fill a large stockpot one-third full with oil and heat over high heat to 375°F.

3. Drain and dry the wings well. Working in batches to avoid crowding, if necessary, fry the wings in the oil until brown and crispy, 15 to 20 minutes. Remove the wings with a flat strainer and transfer them to a large bowl. Add the cheese to the marinade, add the mixture to the wings, and toss well. Serve immediately with the chilled celery.

IN THIS CHAPTER

SYRUPS

To most cooks, a syrup is something you pour over pancakes or use to make a sundae. I love to use sweet syrups, but those here, made by reducing soy sauce, vinegars, and citrus juices to blend and intensify their flavors, serve other ends. Three-Vinegar Syrup, made with balsamic, rice wine, and Chinese vinegars, adds sweet-tart flavor to Seared Halibut with Warm Fennel and Yellow Finn Potato Salad, a great dish of roasted beef tenderloin served with glazed leeks, where it beautifully balances sweetness with refreshing tart flavors. Soy–Kaffir Lime Syrup, my take on Indonesian kecap manis, is a great brush-on glaze for meat and poultry and also works beautifully for fish as in Soy–Kaffir Lime Glazed Salmon with Lime Sushi Rice, among other dishes in this chapter. Similarly, Carrot-Chipotle Syrup, a carrot-juice reduction warmed with chipotle in adobo, does great things in Seared Scallops with Glazed Carrots and Onion Compote, and in sweet potato pies you cook like a gratin (no crust to fuss with!), among other dishes here.

Reductions can also be used as plate drizzles, a restaurant approach you've no doubt encountered when dining out. This isn't only about décor, however. A syrup can add a final note of welcome flavor, as the carrot reduction does in Grilled Shrimp, Bacon, and Pineapple with Carrot-Chipotle Glaze, where it serves as a final "drizzle." In addition to this technique, you'll learn other useful methods in this chapter that will help you create your own "mother" syrups. The rule of thumb: reducing ingredients intensifies their flavors; "lift" these reductions with a bit of oil, and you've got instant flavor-makers.

MASTER RECIPE

THREE-VINEGAR SYRUP

This vinegar reduction, which adds intriguing sweet-tart flavor to dishes, takes advantage of the fact that when balsamic vinegar is cooked down, its inherent sweetness is intensified. Three-Vinegar Syrup combines the complex flavors of balsamic, rice wine, and Chinese black vinegars. It does wonders for beef and seafood, but it can also be used to intensify the taste and aroma of sweet foods including fruit, or as a dessert sauce; I serve it over vanilla ice cream with great success. And because it *is* syrupy, you can use it decoratively, too, to beautify plates while adding a flavor accent.

Makes a scant $1/2$ cup
Lasts 4 weeks, refrigerated

2 cups balsamic vinegar
2 cups rice wine vinegar
$1/2$ cup Chinese black vinegar, or an additional $1/2$ cup balsamic vinegar
plus 1 piece of star anise

In a nonreactive saucepan, combine the vinegars (and star anise, if using) and bring to a simmer over low heat. Continue to simmer until the mixture is reduced by about 80 percent and thickly syrupy, 1 to $1^{1}/2$ hours. (If using the star anise, remove it after the first 30 minutes of cooking.) To test for proper consistency, drizzle a little of the syrup on a chilled plate. It should keep its shape when the plate is tilted. Use or store.

GREEN PEPPERCORN BEEF TENDERLOIN WITH VINEGAR-GLAZED LEEKS

I remember, as a kid, going to a local Ponderosa Steak House. With your steak, you had a choice of grilled onions or canned mushrooms (for fifty cents extra). I always went for the onions, and so enjoyed and came to love the classic combo of beef and onions. Years later I discovered leeks, superior in every way to plain onions when paired with juicy tenderloin. Green peppercorns and the Three-Vinegar Syrup add even more tempting flavor to this easy dish.

BEVERAGE TIP

Grape type
Sangiovese

Characteristics
Ripe cherries, raisin, cedar, tobacco, cocoa

Recommendations
Castello Banfi
Brunello di Montalcino
Tuscany, Italy

Serves 4

4 beef tenderloin filets, 6 to 8 ounces each
Kosher salt to taste
$1/2$ cup cracked green peppercorns
3 tablespoons grapeseed or canola oil
3 leeks, white and light green parts, root-ends trimmed, cut into $1/2$-inch rings, washed, and dried (see Ming's Tip, page 22)
Freshly ground black pepper to taste
5 tablespoons Three-Vinegar Syrup (page 162)
2 tablespoons unsalted butter

1. Preheat the oven to 525°F.

2. Season the beef with salt and coat on both sides with the $1/2$ cup of peppercorns (you may have some left over). Heat an ovenproof sauté pan over medium-high heat. Add 2 tablespoons of the oil and swirl to coat the pan. Sauté the filets on one side until well colored, 2 to 3 minutes, turn them, and transfer the pan to the oven. Roast until the beef is cooked, 6 to 8 minutes for medium-rare.

3. Meanwhile, heat a second sauté pan over high heat. Add the remaining tablespoon of oil and swirl to coat the pan. Add the leeks, season with salt and ground black pepper, and sauté until the leeks are soft, 3 to 5 minutes. Correct the seasoning. Add 3 tablespoons of the syrup and the butter and toss to coat the leeks evenly.

4. Cut each filet diagonally into 5 slices. Place a mound of leeks on each of 4 plates, arrange a filet next to it, drizzle with the remaining syrup, and serve.

BEVERAGE TIP

Grape type

Tempranillo

Characteristics

Earthy, vanillin oak,
ripe berries

Recommendations

Allende
Rioja Alta, Spain

Montecillo Reserva
Rioja, Spain

MING'S TIPS

To prepare and slice the
fennel, first remove its
fronds and stalks (save
these for another use).
Place the halved and
cored bulbs flat side down
on your work surface and
slice by hand or with a
mechanical slicer.

You can prepare the
fennel ahead; keep it well
covered in ice water in the
refrigerator. When you're
ready to use it, spin it dry,
or drain it and dry it with
paper towels, then toss it
with the lemon juice.

SEARED HALIBUT WITH WARM FENNEL AND YELLOW FINN POTATO SALAD

I don't usually try to simplify Blue Ginger dishes for home cooks, feeling they tend to lose something in the translation. But this all-in-one crowd pleaser is an exception. It was originally prepared with artichokes; I then realized that the warm fennel and potato salad without the artichokes were sufficient accompaniments. In fact, I like it better now that's it's pared down and more approachable.

Serves 4

Canola oil for cooking, plus 2 tablespoons
4 large unpeeled Yellow Finn potatoes, cut into $1/2$-inch dice and well dried
Kosher salt and freshly ground black pepper to taste
4 halibut fillets, 6 to 8 ounces each, skin removed
2 fennel bulbs, halved, cored, sliced $1/16$ inch thick, and tossed with the juice of 1 lemon to prevent browning
2 tablespoons chopped fresh chives
5 tablespoons Three-Vinegar Syrup (page 162)

1. Preheat the oven to 200°F. Line a large ovenproof plate with paper towels and set aside.

2. Heat a large nonstick sauté pan over high heat. Add enough oil to fill the pan by $1/4$ inch and heat. Add the potatoes and season with salt and pepper. Shake the pan to ensure that no potatoes are sticking, cover, and sauté until the potatoes have softened and colored on the bottom, 3 to 4 minutes. Turn the potatoes and continue to sauté until evenly colored, 3 to 4 minutes more. Transfer the potatoes with their cooking oil to the reserved plate and put them in the oven to keep hot.

3. Wipe the pan. Season the halibut with salt and pepper. Reheat the pan over high heat. Add the 2 tablespoons of oil and swirl to coat the pan. Add the halibut and sauté, turning once, until brown and just cooked through, 6 to 10 minutes total, depending on the fish's thickness.

4. Meanwhile, in a large bowl, combine the fennel and the potatoes with their oil, the chives, and 3 tablespoons of the Three-Vinegar Syrup. Season with salt and pepper and toss gently to combine.

5. Garnish 4 serving plates with some of the remaining syrup. Mound the potato mixture on each and drizzle the remaining syrup over the portions. Top with the halibut and serve.

MASTER RECIPE

TRY IT
This is a great brush-on glaze for meat, poultry, and vegetables. Or drizzle it on them after cooking.

To make a delicious dressing for composed salads, mix 2 tablespoons of the syrup with the juice of 2 lemons and a heaping teaspoon of Dijon mustard, then whisk in ¼ cup of grapeseed or canola oil.

Make meatloaf special by garnishing plates with the syrup before serving.

MING'S TIP
Turbinado sugar is available in some supermarkets and most health food stores but you can use regular light brown sugar instead.

SOY–KAFFIR LIME SYRUP

This reduction, which blends the sweetness of caramely turbinado sugar with the exotic flavor of kaffir lime, is my version of kecap manis, sweet Indonesian soy sauce. Kecap manis is part of the recipe, but the mixture is made more exciting with the addition of the other flavor notes.

Makes 3 cups
Lasts 2 weeks, refrigerated

3 cups turbinado sugar, or brown sugar
2 cups naturally brewed soy sauce
2 cups kecap manis, or 2 more cups soy sauce plus 2 more cups sugar
1 cup fresh lime juice
8 kaffir lime leaves (fresh or frozen), crushed, or the zest of 1 large lime

In a nonreactive medium saucepan, combine the sugar, soy sauce, kecap manis, lime juice, and kaffir leaves. Bring to a very gentle simmer over medium heat, uncovered, being careful not to boil. Reduce the liquid by about half or until syrupy, 30 to 45 minutes. (Test it for proper consistency by drizzling some in a line on a cold plate; it should resemble maple syrup.) Using a rubber spatula, press the syrup through a fine sieve to strain out the leaves. Let the syrup cool and use or store.

BEVERAGE TIP

Grape type
Cabernet Franc

Characteristics
Lively, Herbs de
Provence, cran-grape

Recommendations
Domaine Charles Joguet
Chinon, France

MING'S TIPS

To dry the cauliflower,
or any blanched veg-
etable, quickly, use a
salad spinner.

The easiest way to
break cauliflower into
florets is, first, to
remove any green
leaves and halve the
head vertically. Then,
with a paring knife,
core the halves and cut
away the stem portions.
All the florets will fall
from the stem halves
and can be easily sepa-
rated with the knife if
large, or by hand.

SOY–KAFFIR LIME CHICKEN BREAST WITH GLAZED CAULIFLOWER

Cauliflower is an underused vegetable, which is a real shame. I love it in soups and in dishes like this that feature the vegetable's crisp texture and mild, delicious flavor. Here, cauliflower is baked with chicken and drizzled with Soy–Kaffir Lime Syrup, which ties all the flavors together. Because of the vegetable's texture, you could think of this as a potato-less chicken with potatoes: You get a satisfying "starchy" accompaniment without all those potato carbs.

Remember not to over-blanch the cauliflower. You want it crisp.

Serves 4

Kosher salt to taste
1 large cauliflower, or 2 medium, broken into small florets
4 large boneless chicken breasts, skin on
Freshly ground black pepper to taste
2 tablespoons grapeseed or canola oil
1 bunch of scallions, white and green parts separated, thinly sliced
¼ cup Soy–Kaffir Lime Syrup (page 168), plus additional for drizzling
1 tablespoon toasted sesame seeds (see Ming's Tip, page 239)

1. Fill a large bowl with water and add ice. Bring a large pot of salted water to a boil and add the cauliflower. Blanch it for about 2 minutes; the cauliflower should be al dente. Using a slotted spoon, transfer the cauliflower to the bowl. When cold, drain and dry well.

2. Preheat the oven to 500°F. Season the chicken very lightly with salt and pepper.

3. Heat a large, ovenproof sauté pan over high heat. Add the oil and swirl to coat the pan. Add the chicken, skin side down, and sauté until brown, 5 to 7 minutes. Turn and scatter the cauliflower and the white parts of the scallions around the chicken. Brush the chicken and drizzle the cauliflower with ¼ cup of the syrup. Transfer the pan to the oven and bake until the chicken is just cooked through, 6 to 8 minutes.

4. Lightly drizzle 4 serving plates with additional syrup. Place a small mound of the cauliflower on each of the plates, top with the chicken, and pour the pan juices over it. Garnish with the scallion greens and sesame seeds and serve.

BEVERAGE TIP

Grape type

Chardonnay

Characteristics

Buttery, vanillin oak,
ripe pear and
pineapple

Recommendations

Kistler
Sonoma Coast,
California

MING'S TIP

Rice cookers make great
rice. Used by millions of
Asians, who know about
rice, the cookers are foolproof and almost effort-
less to operate.

SOY–KAFFIR LIME GLAZED SALMON WITH LIME SUSHI RICE

This is a dish for teriyaki salmon lovers, and for anyone else who enjoys the combination of smoky grilled fish with a tart-sweet glaze. Here, the traditional teriyaki orange flavoring is replaced with lime, and the fish is served with lime-spiked rice. This is delicious—and incredibly easy to make.

Serves 4

4 salmon fillets, 6 to 8 ounces each, preferably center-cut, with skin
Kosher salt and freshly ground black pepper to taste
1/4 cup Soy–Kaffir Lime Syrup (page 168)
2 cups cooked sushi rice (see Ming's Tip, page 147)
Juice of 3 limes
2 tablespoons minced fresh chives

1. If your broiling element is in the oven, place a heavy baking sheet on an oven rack and preheat. Otherwise, preheat the broiler with an unperforated broiling tray in place.

2. Lightly season the salmon with salt and pepper. Spray the hot baking sheet with nonstick cooking spray and place the salmon, flesh side down, on the sheet. Broil the salmon until crispy and colored, 4 to 5 minutes. Turn and using a pastry brush, brush the top and sides of the salmon with some of the syrup and continue broiling until done, 4 to 5 minutes for medium-rare.

3. Meanwhile, in a medium bowl, combine the hot rice with the lime juice and chives, and mix gently. Mound some rice on each serving plate. Brush the salmon with some of the remaining syrup and, using a metal spatula, place it on top of the rice. Drizzle with the remaining syrup and serve.

SEARED TUNA WITH SOBA NOODLE SALAD AND SOY–KAFFIR LIME SYRUP

Anyone who likes Japanese food has enjoyed raw tuna with the usual dips. This takeoff pairs glazed seared tuna—I like it still slightly raw at the center, but suit yourself—with a sprightly soba noodle salad. This is a popular dish at Blue Ginger, where we wrap the noodles in nori seaweed to make maki rolls, but it's every bit as good, and more quickly prepared, this way.

Serves 4

Four 6- to 8-ounce pieces of center-cut Ahi tuna (about 3 by 2 by 2 inches each)
Kosher salt and freshly ground black pepper to taste
2 tablespoons grapeseed or canola oil, plus 1/3 cup
2 teaspoons wasabi powder
1/4 cup rice wine vinegar
1/4 cup Soy–Kaffir Lime Syrup (page 168)
1 hothouse (seedless) cucumber, washed and cut into 3-inch julienne
1/2 pound blanched soba noodles (page 15)

1. Season the tuna with salt and pepper. Heat a sauté pan over high heat. Add the 2 tablespoons of oil and swirl to coat the pan. Add the tuna and sauté, turning, until cooked, 2 to 3 minutes total for rare.

2. Meanwhile, in a large bowl, combine the wasabi and vinegar and whisk until smooth. Whisk in 1 tablespoon of the syrup and then the 1/3 cup oil to make an emulsion. Season with salt and pepper. Transfer the vinaigrette to a small bowl.

3. In the same large bowl, combine the cucumbers and noodles. Add half the vinaigrette and toss to coat; if necessary, add more vinaigrette. Correct the seasoning with salt and pepper.

4. Garnish 4 large dinner plates with the remaining syrup and vinaigrette. Place a mound of the soba salad on each plate. Cut each piece of tuna into 3 slices and arrange next to the salad. Serve.

MASTER RECIPE

TRY IT

This makes a great sauce for most seafood, particularly for cod, bass, scallops, and lobster.

Drizzle the syrup over vegetable medleys; it adds a hint of sweetness and "marries" all the flavors.

For extra flavor, use the syrup to encircle servings of seafood risotto.

MING'S TIPS

Juicing fresh carrots with a juicer is best, but the store-bought juice works well, too.

To ensure the syrup doesn't separate, add the oil to the blender very slowly at first. As soon as thickening occurs, add the oil more quickly. (The initial slow addition allows the mixture to combine; the faster addition prevents the mixture from getting too hot, which can cause it to separate.)

CARROT-CHIPOTLE SYRUP

When you reduce fruit and vegetable juices, they become more intensely themselves. Treated that way, they're perfect flavoring bases; witness this syrup made from reduced carrot juice and smoky-hot chipotle in adobo. I fell in love with that seasoning when I cooked in Santa Fe; here, it complements the reduction's sweetness beautifully, making the syrup a very tasty, as well as useful, ingredient.

Makes 1 cup
Lasts 2 weeks, refrigerated

2 quarts fresh carrot juice
1 teaspoon chopped chipotle in adobo
3/4 cup grapeseed oil
Kosher salt and freshly ground black pepper to taste

1. In a large nonreactive saucepan, bring the carrot juice to a gentle simmer over low heat. Reduce the juice until all the liquid is evaporated, leaving a wet residue, about 45 minutes.

2. With a heat-resistant rubber spatula, scrape the residue from the pan and transfer it to a blender. Add the chipotle in adobo, and blend at high speed. With the machine running, drizzle in the oil very slowly at first until the mixture is emulsified, then add the oil more quickly to prevent the sauce from breaking. Season with salt and pepper. Use or store.

SEARED SCALLOPS WITH GLAZED CARROTS AND ONION COMPOTE

Next to crab, scallops are my favorite seafood. For this dish, they're seared and served with a gingery carrot and onion "compote" whose natural sweetness is enhanced by Carrot-Chipotle Syrup. The smoky heat of the syrup adds bite while giving the scallops a flavor reminiscent of Chinese smoked scallops. This is a great, simple dish.

Serves 4

2 tablespoons unsalted butter
1 large red onion, cut into 1-inch dice
One 1-pound bag of peeled baby carrots
One teaspoon powdered ginger
Kosher salt and freshly ground black pepper to taste
1¼ pounds large sea scallops, muscle removed, if necessary
2 tablespoons grapeseed or canola oil
¼ cup Carrot-Chipotle Syrup (page 176)

1. Heat a large sauté pan over medium heat. Add 1 tablespoon of the butter, and when it has melted, swirl to coat the pan. Add the onion and carrots and cook the vegetables just until they're no longer raw, about 2 minutes. Add the ginger and season with salt and pepper. Reduce the heat to low and add ½ cup of water. Cover and cook until the carrots are soft and the water has evaporated, about 10 minutes. Keep warm.

2. Meanwhile, season the scallops with salt and pepper. Heat a large, nonstick sauté pan over high heat. Add the oil and swirl to coat the pan. Add the scallops and sear them, without moving them, until brown and just cooked through, turning once, 5 to 6 minutes total.

3. Add the remaining tablespoon of butter to the carrot mixture along with 2 tablespoons of the Carrot–Chipotle Syrup. Toss well and correct the seasoning with salt and pepper. Place mounds of the carrot mixture on 4 large dinner plates, surround with sautéed scallops, drizzle with the remaining syrup, and serve.

BEVERAGE TIP
Grape type
Chenin Blanc

Characteristics
Slightly sweet, ripe peaches, mandarin orange, wet stone

Recommendations
Chalbon Baumond Loire, France

MING'S TIPS
Scallops sometimes come with a white nub-like muscle attached. Pull it off with your fingers and discard.

I like cooking scallops to medium doneness, with a bit of translucency at their centers. But cooking them all the way through is fine also; just don't *overcook* them or they'll be tough.

SWEET POTATO POT PIE WITH CARROT-CHIPOTLE SYRUP

I'll come clean: As a kid I not only ate, but thoroughly enjoyed, frozen chicken pot pies. This all-vegetable version not only dispenses with the meat, but replaces the often-gummy crust with a delicate spiced panko "gratin" topping. The syrup does wonders for the potato and celery-root filling.

You can assemble the pies, minus the topping, in advance and refrigerate them for up to a day. (Add the panko right before they go in the oven.) If starting with chilled pies, bake them for 45 minutes rather than the 20 minutes specified. The panko topping should be colored by then; if not, put the crocks under the broiler very briefly.

Serves 4

2 tablespoons grapeseed or canola oil
1 large onion, cut into 1/2-inch dice
4 ounces peeled baby carrots
4 celery stalks, cut into 1-inch lengths
2 large sweet potatoes, peeled and cut into 1-inch dice
1 large celery root (celeriac), or 1 additional sweet potato, peeled and cut into 1-inch dice
Kosher salt and freshly ground black pepper to taste
2 cups homemade or store-bought vegetable broth or Master Chicken Broth (page 192)
1 tablespoon cornstarch well blended with 1 tablespoon water
1/2 cup Carrot-Chipotle Syrup (page 176)
1 1/2 cups Spiced Panko Bread Crumbs (page 218), regular panko (Japanese bread crumbs), or unseasoned bread crumbs

1. Preheat the oven to 375°F.

2. Heat a large stockpot over high heat. Add the oil and swirl to coat the pot. Add the onion and sauté, stirring, until soft, about 2 minutes. Add the carrots, celery, sweet potatoes, and celery root. Season with salt and pepper and sauté 4 minutes more. Add the broth and simmer until the liquid is reduced by half, about 15 minutes. Correct the seasoning, add the cornstarch mixture, and simmer until lightly thickened, about 3 minutes more.

3. Add 1/4 cup of the syrup, mix, divide the filling among four 6- to 8-ounce crocks or other baking dishes, and top with the panko. Transfer the crocks to a baking sheet and bake until the filling is bubbling hot and the panko is well colored, about 20 minutes. Drizzle the pot pies with the remaining syrup and serve.

GRILLED SHRIMP, BACON, AND PINEAPPLE WITH CARROT-CHIPOTLE GLAZE

Who can resist the combination of naturally sweet seafood and salty smoked bacon? I've never been able to since I had my first bacon-wrapped scallop brochette years ago. This version, which substitutes shrimp for scallops, also includes pineapple, a perfect match for the other ingredients; the syrup "marries" everything.

Serve this one with jasmine rice.

Serves 4

12 bacon slices
12 jumbo shrimp, partially peeled and butterflied
1 small pineapple, peeled, cored, and cut into 1-inch dice
Kosher salt and freshly ground black pepper to taste
6 cups cooked jasmine rice
¼ cup Carrot-Chipotle Syrup (page 176)
2 tablespoons chopped chives (optional)

Eight 5-inch wooden skewers, soaked in water for 1 hour

1. Prepare an outdoor grill and heat to hot. Alternatively, preheat the broiler.

2. Lay the bacon on your work surface. Place a shrimp on each slice toward the top. Curl each shrimp around a pineapple chunk, then roll it tightly in the bacon. Skewer the shrimp with 2 parallel skewers through the head and tail, placing 3 shrimp on each pair of skewers. Repeat to make 3 more skewers. Season the wrapped shrimp lightly with salt and pepper. If using an outdoor grill, spray the grid with nonstick cooking spray. If using a broiler, cover the pan and insertion with foil for easy cleanup. Grill or broil the shrimp until the bacon is brown and crispy and the shrimp are cooked through, turning once, 5 to 6 minutes total.

3. Mound the rice on 4 dinner plates and top each with a skewer. Drizzle the syrup over the shrimp and around the plate, garnish with chives, if using, and serve.

IN THIS CHAPTER

BROTHS

As a chef-to-be, one of the first things I was taught was stock-making. But I didn't have to go to school to learn that chicken broth, integral to Chinese cooking, is the building block of many sauces and soups. My East-West versions of chicken and beef broths don't differ that much from traditional versions in terms of technique because there's just no better way to make them than the classic way. But my Eastern additions—oxtail and pork to the meat broth, and ginger, star anise, and flavor-deepening soy sauce to the chicken broth—make them unique. The broths are great flavor sources in dishes like Five-Spice Beef Noodle Soup, Grilled Lamb Loin Chops with Wild Mushroom Ragout, and the super-easy, super-good Ginger-Poached Whole Chicken.

I wish more cooks would get hip to dashi, the fundamental Japanese stock. Quickly made (unlike other stocks), it adds smoky, sea-fresh flavor to a host of dishes like classic Miso Soup with Tofu and Nori and Rock Shrimp Miso Risotto with Spinach, my East-West take on the classic Italian dish. It's also a boon to those who want to keep their cooking meatless. Most cooks know that having stocks on hand is culinary money-in-the-bank; here, they're a major investment.

MASTER MEAT BROTH

TRY IT

Some of the best dishes begin with broth, an uncomplicated-to-prepare base that adds depth of flavor to many preparations. This meat broth takes its inspiration from classic French *jus de veau*, a lightly thickened broth made from veal bones. To that basic ingredient, I've added oxtail and pork (my Asian touch), which slightly sweetens and rounds out the flavor. Ginger and soy sauce are also included. This broth is versatile by definition; you'll find dozens of ways to put it to good use.

TRY IT
The broth is, of course, a basic sauce component. For the simplest sauce I can think of, reduce 1 quart of the broth by three quarters. Float 1 tablespoon of extra-virgin olive oil over the reduction and use it to sauce steaks or pork.

The broth makes a great beef and vegetable soup, but it's also the basis of delicious puréed soups, like one made from regular and "wild" mushrooms such as cèpes, porcinis, and chanterelles.

MING'S TIPS
I like to freeze the broth in ice-cube trays. When it's solid, I pop the cubes into a freezer bag, from which I can take as much or as little as I need.

If you have difficulty getting pork bones, you can increase the quantity of veal bones by their equivalent amount, 5 pounds.

Makes about 5 quarts
Lasts 1 week refrigerated, 3 months frozen

5 pounds oxtail
10 pounds veal bones
5 pounds pork bones (you can include pork shank or trotters)
$1/4$ cup grapeseed or canola oil
Kosher salt and freshly ground black pepper to taste
1 head of celery, rinsed and coarsely chopped
3 large carrots, rinsed and coarsely chopped
3 large onions, coarsely chopped
1 bottle red wine
1 tablespoon whole black peppercorns
2 bay leaves
Three $1/4$-inch slices of peeled fresh ginger
$1/4$ cup tomato paste
$1/4$ cup naturally brewed soy sauce

1. Preheat the oven to 375°F.

2. In a large roasting pan or 2 smaller pans, combine the oxtail and the veal and pork bones and toss with the oil. Season with salt and pepper, and roast the bones, turning them from time to time, until dark brown, about 2 hours.

3. Transfer the bones to a large stockpot. Pour off as much fat as possible, and transfer the pan(s) to stovetop burners over high heat. Add the celery, carrots, and onions and sauté, stirring, until brown, 5 to 7 minutes. Add the wine, scrape the bottom of the pan with a wooden spoon to incorporate flavorful bits, and allow the wine to reduce by three quarters. Transfer the mixture to the stockpot. Add the peppercorns, bay leaves, ginger, tomato paste, and soy sauce. Add sufficient water to cover the bones by about 3 inches, decrease the heat to low, and simmer very gently (the liquid should barely bubble) until the stock is dark and reduced by about one third, 8 to 12 hours or overnight.

4. Strain the stock. Use, or allow to cool to room temperature and store.

FIVE-SPICE BEEF NOODLE SOUP

A good, warming bowl of beef noodle soup: Is there anything better? The key to making a standout soup is a good stock base, which your supply of Master Meat Broth provides.

Like the Vietnamese *pho* on which this soup is based, this recipe features thin slices of raw beef, which are added just before the soup is served. The beef cooks right away in the hot soup and, along with fresh spinach leaves, makes this dish very special.

BEVERAGE TIP

Grape type
Sangiovese

Characteristics
Juicy, cherry, raspberry, fresh

Recommendations
Avignonesi
Rosso di Montepulciano, Italy

Serves 4 to 6

8 ounces beef tenderloin (filet mignon)
2 tablespoons grapeseed or canola oil
2 leeks, white and light green parts, thinly sliced, well washed and dried
  (see Ming's Tip, page 22)
1 tablespoon five-spice or eight-spice powder (see page 13)
Kosher salt and freshly ground black pepper to taste
6 cups Master Meat Broth (page 184)
1 pound Shanghai noodles or other thick wheat noodle, blanched (page 15)
8 ounces baby spinach leaves
¼ cup fresh cilantro leaves (stems discarded)

1. At least 4 hours in advance, or overnight, wrap the beef in plastic wrap and freeze. When ready to make the soup, remove the beef from the freezer, allow it to defrost for 20 to 30 minutes, and slice it as thin as possible. (Alternatively, slice the beef ¼ inch thick, place it between sheets of plastic wrap, and pound the meat with a meat pounder or with the flat side of a heavy pan until paper thin.) Refrigerate the beef until ready to use.

2. Heat a stockpot over medium heat. Add the oil and swirl to coat the bottom of the pot. Add the leeks and cook, stirring, until translucent, about 2 minutes. Add the five-spice powder and season with salt and pepper. Add the broth and bring to a boil. Add the noodles and return to a boil. Correct the seasoning with salt and pepper.

3. Divide the spinach among 4 large soup or pasta bowls. Using tongs, add equal portions of the noodles to the bowls, then add the broth and equal portions of the beef (which will cook instantly in the hot soup). Garnish with the cilantro and serve.

EAST-WEST BEEF AND BEAN STEW

Stews can be dull, but this beef and bean version gets taste buds tingling. That's because it contains fiery sambal as well as ginger. This is a meal-in-one dish; just add a side salad and some crusty bread.

Serves 4

3 tablespoons grapeseed or canola oil
2 pounds beef brisket, cut into 1-inch cubes
Kosher salt and freshly ground black pepper to taste
2 large red onions, cut into 1/2-inch dice
2 carrots, peeled and sliced 1/4 inch thick
3 celery stalks, sliced 1/4 inch thick
2 cups dried white beans, soaked overnight, or canned, well rinsed
1 tablespoon peeled and minced fresh ginger
1 tablespoon Traditional Spicy Sambal (page 56) or store-bought sambal
2 quarts Master Meat Broth (page 184)

1. Heat a stockpot over high heat. Add 2 tablespoons of the oil and swirl to coat the bottom of the pot. Add the beef, season with salt and pepper, and sear on all sides until well colored, 4 to 5 minutes. Transfer to a plate and set aside.

2. Reheat the pot over high heat, add the remaining tablespoon of oil, and swirl to coat the bottom of the pot. Add the onions, carrots, and celery and season with salt and pepper. Sauté until soft, about 3 minutes. Add the beans, ginger, sambal, broth, and beef and correct the seasoning with salt and pepper. Bring to a simmer, reduce the heat, and cook until the beans are very soft, about 45 minutes. Correct the seasoning again and serve.

BEVERAGE TIP
Grape type
Merlot

Characteristics
Ripe plum, roasted
eggplant, roasted
spiced meat,
suppleness, elegant

Recommendations
Chalk Hill,
Estate Bottle
Sonoma County,
California

GRILLED LAMB LOIN CHOPS
WITH WILD MUSHROOM RAGOUT

I've mentioned that Master Meat Broth makes a great base for a sauce, and here it does just that, adding flavor intensity to a mixed mushroom ragout served with grilled lamb chops. Because lamb has such deep flavor, the ragout–chop combination is a match made in heaven. And you get those wonderful, meaty bones to gnaw on.

Serves 4

2 tablespoons extra-virgin olive oil
4 shallots, sliced ¼ inch thick
8 ounces shiitake mushrooms, stemmed and quartered
8 ounces button mushrooms, quartered
8 ounces oyster mushrooms, torn in half
Kosher salt and freshly ground black pepper to taste
1 bottle dry red wine
2 quarts Master Meat Broth (page 184)
1 tablespoon minced fresh thyme or 1 teaspoon dried thyme
8 loin lamb chops, about ¾ inch thick
Four 1-inch-thick slices of baguette, toasted
1 tablespoon fresh mint cut into thin ribbons

1. Prepare an outdoor grill and heat to hot. Alternatively, preheat the broiler.

2. Heat a large saucepan over high heat. Add the oil and swirl to coat the pan. Add the shallots and sauté until soft, about 2 minutes. Add the mushrooms, season with salt and pepper, and sauté until soft, about 3 minutes. Add the wine, scraping the bottom of the pan with a wooden spoon to incorporate flavorful bits. Add the broth and thyme and reduce the heat and simmer until the mixture is sauce-like, 45 to 60 minutes. Correct the seasoning with salt and pepper and keep warm.

3. Spray the grill grid or broiler pan with nonstick cooking spray. Season the chops with salt and pepper and grill or broil, turning once, until cooked, 4 to 5 minutes per side for medium-rare.

4. Divide the baguette slices among 4 plates and top with all but ½ cup of the mushroom ragout. Place 2 chops on each plate. Drizzle with the remaining ragout, garnish with the mint, and serve.

MASTER RECIPE

TRY IT

Use the broth to cook rice and for risottos, like the one on page 202.

You've probably heard chicken soup called Jewish penicillin. Now there's Chinese penicillin, too: steep 8 (a lucky number to the Chinese) slices of ginger in 4 cups of hot broth for 30 minutes, strain it out, and serve the soup. (You can also add ginseng.) The soup's great for colds and sore throats, I've found.

For instant poultry "sauces," use about 1 cup of the broth to deglaze the pan in which chicken, turkey, or meat has cooked. While the broth cooks down, mix 1 teaspoon of cornstarch with an additional 2 tablespoons of broth, and stir this slurry into the pan to thicken the sauce lightly.

MING'S TIP

You'll want to use chicken bones, rather than meaty parts, to make the broth. Ask your butcher for the bones or buy chicken wings and backs at the supermarket. If you live near a Chinatown, you can get chicken feet, which add a rich gelatinous quality to your broth.

MASTER CHICKEN BROTH

For me, chicken broth is the soul of Chinese cooking and an indispensable East–West ingredient. We use it for innumerable dishes, from soups and stir-frys to braises and sauces, including the dishes that follow.

What makes my version different from most is the addition of star anise, ginger, and soy sauce, which not only salts the broth, but provides depth of flavor. This chicken broth is so simple to make, and keeps so beautifully, it's almost a shame not to have some on hand at all times. If you don't want to bother freezing the broth, you can extend its refrigerated life by boiling it every 5 days or so, cooling it, and then re-refrigerating it. That way, it will last 2 to 3 weeks.

Makes about 7 quarts
Lasts about 1 week refrigerated (but see above) or 1 month frozen

15 pounds chicken bones, such as backs, wings, carcasses, and feet
1 head of celery, rinsed and coarsely chopped
3 large carrots, rinsed and coarsely chopped
3 large onions, coarsely chopped
1 teaspoon black peppercorns
2 bay leaves
2 sprigs of fresh thyme
1/4 bunch of fresh flat-leaf parsley
1 star anise
Two 1/4-inch-thick slices of ginger cut lengthwise from a 2- to 3-inch-long piece
2 tablespoons naturally brewed soy sauce

1. Rinse the bones and place them in a large stockpot. Add enough cold water to cover the bones by 3 to 4 inches and bring to a simmer over medium heat. Skim the scum that rises to the surface as it appears, reduce the heat to low, and simmer until chicken fat rises to the surface, about 1 hour. (Ladle the fat into a bowl and reserve for other cooking.)

2. Add the celery, carrots, onions, peppercorns, bay leaves, thyme, parsley, star anise, ginger, and soy sauce. Continue to simmer until the stock is well flavored, 3 to 4 hours more. Strain the stock and allow to cool to room temperature. Use or store.

BEVERAGE TIP

Grape type
Sauvignon Blanc
and Sémillon

Characteristics
Lime, lanolin,
mineral, crisp

Recommendations
Chateau la Louvière
Pessac Leognan,
Bordeaux, France

MING'S TIP
The broth in which the
chickens are cooked is
delicious and can be
used again. If not
frozen, boil it first to
ensure its safety.

GINGER-POACHED WHOLE CHICKEN

Based on an old Chinese method, this dish produces perfectly cooked chicken, and it couldn't be easier to do. All you do is put chicken in a pot with broth and additional flavorings, cover and partially cook it, then remove the pot from the heat. The covered bird finishes cooking in the hot liquid and emerges tender and delicious—and almost fat free, as the fat renders into the broth.

Serve this with crusty bread.

Serves 4

Two 2- to 3-pound chickens, preferably kosher or free-range
Kosher salt and freshly ground black pepper to taste
Eight 1/4-inch-thick slices of peeled fresh ginger cut lengthwise from a 2- to 3-inch-long piece
1 bunch of scallions, white and green parts, thinly sliced
1/2 cup packed Thai basil or regular basil leaves
4 quarts Master Chicken Broth (page 192) or low-sodium canned chicken broth
2 large carrots, peeled and finely shredded

1. Season the chickens inside and out with salt and pepper. In a pot large enough to fit the chickens completely submerged in liquid, combine the chickens, breast sides up, with the ginger, scallions, basil, and broth. Cover and bring to a low simmer over medium heat. Reduce the heat to low and simmer for 30 minutes.

2. Lift the cover, add the carrots, cover the pot, and remove from the heat. Allow to stand for 30 minutes or up to 1 hour for the chicken to finish cooking. (Do not lift the lid during this time or cooking heat will be dissipated. The chicken won't overcook, even if left for the maximum time.) Remove the chicken, carve, and serve. (Strain the broth, cool to room temperature, and store for future use.)

LEMONGRASS COCONUT CHICKEN SOUP

This delicious soup is based on a traditional Thai dish, *tom yung gai*. It features what I think of as the definitive Thai flavoring, lemongrass, combined with chicken, coconut milk, and, for heat, sambal.

I've followed the time-honored Thai method, and left large pieces of lemongrass in the soup, but you can strain them out before serving, if you like. (If you leave them in, you might want to warn diners that they're not to be eaten.)

This works beautifully as a first course, or serve it as a light lunch with a salad dressed with a citrus vinaigrette.

Serves 4

1 tablespoon grapeseed or canola oil
4 lemongrass stalks, pale parts only, crushed with the flat side of a knife
2 medium onions, sliced 1/8 inch thick
2 Thai or serrano chiles, stemmed but not seeded, minced (optional)
2 boneless skinless chicken breasts, cut into 1/4-inch strips
3 tablespoons fish sauce (nam pla)
6 cups Master Chicken Broth (page 192) or low-sodium canned chicken broth
1/2 cup coconut milk
Juice of 2 lemons
Kosher salt and freshly ground black pepper to taste
1 tablespoon thinly sliced scallion greens

Heat a medium saucepan over medium-high heat. Add the oil and swirl to coat the pan. Add the lemongrass, stir, and sweat it, uncovered, for 2 minutes. Add the onions and chiles, if using, and sauté, stirring, for 1 minute. Add the chicken and sauté until opaque, about 1 minute. Add the fish sauce and broth, stir, bring to a simmer, and cook until the liquid is reduced slightly to intensify its flavor, 15 to 20 minutes. Whisk in the coconut milk and lemon juice. Season with salt and pepper, garnish with the scallions, and serve.

BEVERAGE TIP
Depends on main
ingredient to be sauced.

MING"S TIP
As everyone has different
sauce needs, serve the
sauce of the side. I, for
example, like lots of sauce
with my roast; my wife,
Polly, likes less.

SHIITAKE-SCALLION PAN SAUCE

Sauces don't have to elaborate or take hours of simmering to prepare. This simple sauce, made ideally in the pan in which you've roasted poultry, leg of lamb, or prime rib, delivers great flavor, and is made in minutes. You can also prepare it in a pan you've used to sauté steak or chicken breasts.

Makes 3 cups

1 tablespoon cornstarch
3 cups Master Chicken Broth (page 192)
1 tablespoon grapeseed or canola oil, if needed
1 bunch scallions, white and green parts, sliced $1/4$-inch thick
1 cup shiitake mushrooms, sliced $1/4$-inch thick
1 cup dry white wine or red wine
Kosher salt and freshly ground black pepper to taste
Juice of $1/2$ lemon

1. In a small bowl combine the cornstarch with 1 teaspoon of the broth and mix well. Set aside.

2. If using a pan in which a roast has been cooked, remove all but 1 tablespoon fat, and put the pan over medium heat. Alternatively, add the oil to a sauté pan and heat over medium heat. Add the scallions and mushrooms and sauté, stirring, until soft, about 3 minutes. Add the wine and deglaze the pan, scraping up any brown bits. Reduce the wine until about $1/4$ cup remains and add the broth. Bring to a simmer and season with the salt and pepper.

3. Whisk in the cornstarch mixture, and simmer until the mixture is lightly thickened, 3 to 5 minutes. Add the juice and correct the seasoning with the salt and pepper. Serve.

BEVERAGE TIP
Beer

Characteristics
Clean, slight sweetness

Recommendations
Tsingtao
China

HOT AND SOUR SHRIMP SOUP

One of the most frequently enjoyed Chinese dishes in America is hot and sour soup. This version tops the rest, I believe, because of its master broth base and the lack of a cornstarch thickening, which can cloud flavors. Here, you taste every element, and, because I use shrimp instead of the traditional pork, you get soup that's extra light, too.

Serves 4

1 tablespoon grapeseed or canola oil
2 tablespoons peeled and minced fresh ginger
6 scallions, green and white parts separated, sliced 1/16 inch thick
1 pound rock or very small shrimp (U-30 count), rinsed, deveined, and well dried
1 teaspoon ground white pepper, plus additional, if needed
Kosher salt to taste
1/2 cup rice wine vinegar
4 cups Master Chicken Broth (page 192) or low-sodium canned chicken broth
4 ounces silken tofu, cut into 1/2-inch dice

Heat a large saucepan over medium-high heat. Add the oil and swirl to coat the pan. Add the ginger and scallion whites and sauté, stirring, until soft, 2 to 3 minutes. Add the shrimp and pepper, season with salt, and continue to sauté for 2 minutes. Add the vinegar and stir with a wooden spoon, scraping the bottom of the pan with a wooden spoon to incorporate caramelized bits. Add the broth, bring to a simmer, and correct the seasoning with salt. Whisk in the tofu, correct the seasoning with salt and pepper, if you like, and pour into soup bowls. Garnish with the scallion greens and serve.

TRY IT

You can use dashi almost anywhere you'd use chicken stock: in soups, or as a poaching liquid, for example. This is particularly good news for non-meat-eaters (although strict vegetarians will note it contains dried fish flakes).

Cook vegetables or rice in dashi for extra flavor.

If you're feeling under the weather or need a pick-me-up, try sipping a cup of hot dashi. It's a great restorative.

MING'S TIP

Bonito flakes are pinkish flakes used primarily in the preparation of dashi, the Japanese cooking stock. Buy them in bags or boxes in Asian markets that have a rapid turnover, as the flakes deteriorate rapidly.

MASTER DASHI BROTH

As many cooks know, dashi is the fundamental Japanese stock. Made easily from a few simple ingredients, it's the basis of miso soup and an integral part of dishes including *sukiyaki* and *shabu-shabu*. The addition of ginger besides the usual kombu seaweed and bonito flakes makes a dashi that is marvelously smoky without being overpowering. Dashi's a versatile ingredient, and one that more Western cooks ought to learn to use.

Makes about 5 cups
Lasts 2 weeks refrigerated or 1 month frozen

1 large piece of kombu (about 5 by 6 inches or 12 by 2 inches, depending on the shape purchased)
Two ¼-inch-thick slices of fresh peeled ginger cut lengthwise from a 2- to 3-inch-long piece
2 cups dried bonito flakes

1. Clean the kombu by wiping it with a damp cloth. Place the kombu and ginger in a stockpot with 5 cups of cold water and heat over medium heat. Just before the water boils, remove the pot from the heat. Watch carefully; you don't want the water to boil or the dashi will become too strongly flavored.

2. Allow the mixture to stand for 5 minutes, remove the kombu, and return the pot to medium heat. When the broth once again nears the boiling point, remove the pot from the heat and add the bonito flakes. When the flakes sink to the bottom of the pot, strain the dashi through cheesecloth or a fine-mesh strainer. Use or cool and store.

BEVERAGE TIP

Grape type

Arneis

Characteristics

Refreshing,
pineapple-citrus,
slight frizzante

Recommendations

Ceretto

Alba, Italy

MING'S TIP

You can cook the risotto
ahead so there's no last-
minute fussing. Hours in
advance of serving, or
even a day ahead, partially
cook the shrimp, as
directed, and set them
aside, refrigerated. Cook
the rice and spread it on a
large platter. Let it cool
and then, if holding it for
over an hour, refrigerate it,
well covered. Just before
you're ready to serve it,
put it in a saucepan with 2
cups of hot dashi broth
and heat the rice gently,
stirring with a wooden
spoon. Add the shrimp
with the spinach, butter,
and lemon juice, heat
through, and serve.

ROCK SHRIMP MISO RISOTTO WITH SPINACH

This is a full-throttle reworking of Italian risotto using Japanese ingredients. For the traditional Arborio rice, I substitute sushi rice (which becomes every bit as al dente and creamy) plus sake and dashi broth. The result, which also features sweet-fleshed rock shrimp, is a great flavor mix.

Serves 4

4 cups Master Dashi Broth (page 200)
$1/2$ cup blond miso (shiro-miso), plus more, if desired
2 tablespoons grapeseed or canola oil
1 pound rock shrimp or very small shrimp (U-30 count), deveined, rinsed
  and dried
1 tablespoon minced garlic
1 medium onion, cut into $1/8$-inch dice
Kosher salt and freshly ground black pepper to taste
2 cups sushi rice or Arborio rice
$1/2$ cup sake or dry white wine
2 cups baby spinach leaves
2 tablespoons unsalted butter
Juice of 1 lemon

RECIPE CONTINUES

1. In a medium saucepan, bring the broth to a simmer over medium heat. Submerge a small strainer halfway into the broth, add the miso to the broth within the strainer, and whisk to combine the miso and broth. Taste and add more miso, 1 tablespoon at a time, if you want a deeper flavor. Keep hot over low heat.

2. Heat a high-sided medium sauté pan over high heat. Add 1 tablespoon of the oil and swirl to coat the pan. Add the shrimp and sauté, stirring, until the shrimp have just colored (they will be raw in the center), about 2 minutes. Transfer the shrimp to a plate and set aside.

3. Return the pan to the heat. Add the remaining tablespoon of oil and swirl to coat the pan. Add the garlic and onion and sweat, uncovered, for about 2 minutes. Season with salt and pepper. Add the rice and sauté, stirring, until lightly toasted, about 2 minutes. Add the sake, stir, and allow it to evaporate, about 2 minutes. Add the broth mixture, reduce the heat to low, and simmer until the rice has absorbed the broth, about 10 minutes. Do not stir.

4. Return the shrimp to the risotto. Add the spinach, butter, and lemon juice and heat, stirring, until the spinach has wilted and the shrimp have finished cooking, about 4 minutes. Serve immediately.

MISO SOUP WITH TOFU AND NORI

The popularity of miso soup has grown tremendously in America, with good reason. This light but deeply flavorful dish has a smoky, almost meaty taste, but it is made, of course, without meat of any kind. Enhanced here with a hint of ginger for spiciness, and garnished with crisp nori seaweed, the soup is just the thing to begin a meal or to warm you on a cold winter day. It's also great for breakfast.

Serves 4

4 cups Master Dashi Broth (page 200)
$1/2$ cup yellow miso (shinshu-miso), plus more if desired
4 ounces silken tofu, cut into $1/2$-inch dice
2 sheets nori (optional), cut into $1/4$-inch strips
2 tablespoons thinly sliced scallions, green parts only

1. In a medium saucepan, bring the broth to a simmer over medium heat. Submerge a small strainer halfway into the broth, add the miso to the broth within the strainer, and whisk to combine the miso and broth. Taste and add more miso, 1 tablespoon at a time, if you want a deeper flavor.

2. Remove the strainer and add the tofu. Divide the nori, if using, and scallion among greens 4 heated soup bowls. Ladle the soup over and serve.

BEVERAGE TIP

Grape type
Sangiovese

Characteristics
Enticing, amber spice,
violets, subtle tannins,
soft elegant ruby red
fruit, rustic cherry
qualities

Recommendations
Monsanto,
Chianti Classico Riserva
Tuscany, Italy

Antinori,
"Tenute Marchese"
Chianti Classico
Reserva
Tuscany, Italy

BEEF AND ONION "SUKIYAKI"

Of all the Japanese dishes Westerners have tried and enjoyed, sukiyaki—dashi-flavored stir-fried beef with vegetables (and sometimes noodles)—is probably most familiar. In this version, top-grade beef is quickly cooked in a deliciously seasoned broth and served in bowls.

If you can get your butcher to slice prime rib for this, you'll really be in business. But tenderloin is a fine choice too, and is more readily available.

Serve this with steamed rice.

Serves 4

8 ounces rice stick noodles
1 tablespoon grapeseed or canola oil
3 large onions, halved and cut into 1/4-inch dice
1 tablespoon peeled and minced fresh ginger
1/2 cup mirin
2 quarts Master Dashi Broth (page 200)
1/4 cup naturally brewed soy sauce
Kosher salt and freshly ground black pepper to taste
1 pound prime rib, halved lengthwise, or beef tenderloin, sliced paper thin
   (have your butcher do this or see page 15)

1. In a large bowl, soak the noodles in enough hot tap water to cover them generously until soft, about 20 minutes. Drain and set aside.

2. Heat a large sauté pan over high heat. Add the oil and swirl to coat the pan. Add the onions and ginger and sauté, stirring, until the onions have caramelized, about 5 minutes. Add the mirin, stir, and cook until the mirin has reduced by half, 2 to 3 minutes. Add the broth, reduce the heat, and bring to a simmer. Cook until the mixture is reduced slightly, about 10 minutes. Add the soy sauce and noodles and season with salt and pepper.

3. "Float" the beef on the surface of the broth and allow it to cook through, turning once, about 1 minute. Transfer the broth, beef, and noodles to heated bowls and serve.

IN THIS CHAPTER

FIVE-SPICE CHILE TEA RUB

SPICED PANKO BREAD CRUMBS

CITRUS HERBAL TEA RUB

RUBS AND COATINGS

I was speaking with a young cook awhile ago and the subject turned to seasoning rubs. (It's true—cooks spend a lot of time talking about cooking.) My friend thought that rubs began during the 1980s with the popularity of Cajun dishes like blackened redfish. But the Chinese have been rubbing ducks with salt and Szechwan peppercorns mixtures for millennia. My East-West rubs follow that precedent but are unique in their use of another, timeless Asian staple, tea. Five-Spice Chile Tea Rub and Citrus Herbal Tea Rub, made, respectively, with fragrant (and good-for-you) lapsang souchong and green mint teas, add intriguing flavor in dishes like Tea-Rubbed Sirloin with Country Mash, Tea-Rubbed Salmon with Steamed Scallion-Lemon Rice, and Citrus Tea–Rubbed Halibut with Orange-Fennel Orzo Salad. A great discovery: when tea-coated meat is braised, as it is in Tea-Braised Lamb Stew, the tea "brews" in the cooking liquid, adding even more flavor to the dish.

The Japanese bread crumbs called panko are chefs'-choice worldwide because they deliver light, airy breadings with superior crunch. I've upped the panko ante by adding herby flavors to my Spiced Panko Bread Crumbs plus heat, to produce dishes like Asian Meatloaf, which is light, juicy, and spicy, too; a terrific breaded-chicken sandwich; and the best, crispiest soft-shelled crabs ever. As you'll see, rubs (and coatings) have a future as well as a past.

FIVE-SPICE CHILE TEA RUB

I've always been fascinated by the use of tea in cooking. Among tea dishes, tea-smoked duck is probably the most ubiquitous, but there's also green tea–flavored ice cream and pound cake. As part of a seasoning rub, tea adds aromatic flavor to a range of dishes. To compose this example, I started with lapsang souchong tea, revered for its smoky, tobacco-like depths, then added spices, including three kinds of pepper, to complement it. The result is a standout rub you'll use often.

Makes about 6 cups
Lasts 3 weeks, refrigerated

3 cups lapsang souchong tea leaves
$1/2$ cup sea salt or kosher salt
$1/2$ cup red pepper flakes
$1/2$ cup chipotle chile powder
$1/2$ cup dehydrated garlic or regular garlic powder (not garlic salt)
$1/4$ cup cayenne pepper
$1/4$ cup dried chives or onions
$1/4$ cup five-spice powder

Combine all the ingredients in a medium bowl. Use or store.

BEVERAGE TIP
Grape type
Malbec

Characteristics
Tobacco, cedar, cocoa,
plum, earth, cassis

Recommendations
Catena, "Lunlunta"
Vineyards
Mendoza, Argentina

Alamos Ridge, Malbec
Mendoza, Argentina

TEA-RUBBED SIRLOIN WITH COUNTRY MASH

Steak and potatoes is a classic, mouthwatering combo. In this East–West version, steak is coated with the Five-Spice Chile Tea Rub, which "smokes" the meat instantly when it hits the grill. Served with over-the-top creamy mashers, the dish makes diners very, very happy.

Serves 4

1 pound unpeeled baking potatoes, well washed
3 tablespoons unsalted butter, chilled
1 large onion, sliced $1/8$ inch thick
4 garlic cloves, minced
1 cup heavy (whipping) cream
Kosher salt and freshly ground black pepper to taste
$1/2$ cup Five-Spice Chile Tea Rub (page 210)
Four 6- to 8-ounce sirloin steaks
2 to 3 tablespoons grapeseed or canola oil, if needed

1. Preheat the oven to 400°F. Bake the potatoes until tender when tested with a thin skewer, 40 to 60 minutes. Transfer to a large bowl.

2. Meanwhile, heat a medium sauté pan over high heat. Add 1 tablespoon of the butter and, when melted, swirl to coat the pan. Add the onion and garlic and sauté, stirring, until lightly brown, about 3 minutes. Add the cream, bring to a simmer, and cook until the cream is reduced by about one quarter, 5 to 8 minutes.

3. Add the cream mixture to the potatoes and using a hand masher, mash the potatoes to a coarse purée. Add the remaining 2 tablespoons of butter. Season with salt and pepper. Keep warm.

4. Spread the rub on a large plate and coat the steaks on both sides with it. Cover with plastic wrap and allow the steaks to flavor for 15 minutes before cooking them. Heat an outdoor grill to high and spray the grid with nonstick cooking spray. Alternatively, heat a very large, heavy sauté pan, or 2 smaller pans, over high heat. Add the oil and swirl to coat the pan(s).

5. Grill or pan-fry the steaks until done to your liking, 4 to 5 minutes per side for medium-rare. Allow the steaks to rest for 5 minutes. Divide the potatoes among 4 plates. Slice the steaks $1/4$ inch thick and serve with the potatoes.

BEVERAGE TIP

Grape type

Grenache

Syrah

Characteristics

Sweet and sour
cherries, spice box,
earth, roast meats,
cooked berry, slightly
smoky, currant,
complex perfume

Recommendations

Domaine Les Pallières
Gigondas, France

Chateau Saint Cosme
Gigondas, France

TEA-BRAISED LAMB STEW

When tea is added to a braising liquid, as it is in this dish, the tea "brews." Here, this steeping adds tremendous smoky flavor that's a perfect foil for lamb and root vegetables. This is one of those dishes that's delicious right after it's cooked, and even better the next day.

To cut the vegetables easily, see the tips on page 15.

Serves 4

1$^1/_2$ pounds lamb stew meat, preferably shoulder, cut into 1-inch cubes
1 cup Five-Spice Chile Tea Rub (page 210)
3 tablespoons grapeseed or canola oil
2 large onions, cut into 1-inch dice
8 ounces trimmed baby carrots
1 large celery stalk, cut into 1-inch dice
2 cups dry red wine
Kosher salt and freshly ground black pepper, if needed
2 large baking potatoes, cut into 1-inch dice
2 large sweet potatoes, cut into 1-inch dice

1. In a large bowl, combine the lamb and the rub and toss to coat the lamb. Allow the lamb to flavor for 15 minutes.

2. Heat a small stockpot over high heat. Add 2 tablespoons of the oil and swirl to coat the pot. Working in batches if necessary, add the lamb and brown it on all sides; remove the pieces to a plate and set aside. Add the remaining tablespoon of oil to the pot and swirl to coat the bottom. Add the onions, carrots, and celery and sweat for 5 minutes. Add the wine and cook until reduced by half, 6 to 8 minutes. Return the lamb to the pot, add enough water to cover the lamb, and bring it to a simmer. Season, if necessary, with salt and pepper. Continue to simmer until the lamb is tender, 1$^1/_2$ to 2 hours, adding the potatoes in the last 30 minutes. Serve in bowls.

TEA-RUBBED SALMON WITH STEAMED SCALLION-LEMON RICE

Salmon takes beautifully to tea rub, as do all fatty fish. You've no doubt been served fish with lemon for as long as you've eaten fish; here, the lemon goes into a delicious rice accompaniment that's further enhanced by scallions. This is a light, healthful dish that's also ultra-simple.

Serves 4

1 cup Five-Spice Chile Tea Rub (page 210)
4 center-cut skinless salmon fillets, 5 to 6 ounces each
2 tablespoons grapeseed or canola oil
2 cups jasmine rice, washed
Juice and zest of 2 lemons
¼ cup thinly sliced scallions, white and green parts
Pinch of salt

1. Spread the rub on a large plate and coat the salmon in it liberally.

2. Heat a large sauté pan over high heat. Add the oil and swirl to coat the pan. Add the salmon and sauté, turning once, until the salmon is cooked, 3 to 4 minutes per side for medium.

3. Meanwhile, cook the rice in a rice cooker, adding the lemon juice, half the zest, the scallions, and the salt to the water. Alternatively, place the rice in a medium saucepan fitted with a tight lid. Flatten the rice with a palm and without removing your hand, add water until it touches the middle and highest knuckle of your hand. Add the lemon juice, half the zest, the scallions, and the salt, cover, and bring the water to a boil over high heat, 10 to 15 minutes. Reduce the heat to medium and simmer for 30 minutes. Turn off the heat and let the rice stand, covered, to plump, for 20 minutes.

4. Place a small mound of rice on 4 plates (there will be rice left over) and top with the salmon. Garnish with the remaining zest and serve.

BEVERAGE TIP

Grape type
Marsanne, Ronssane, Viognier, Grenache Blanc

Characteristics
Aromatic, peach, pear, honeysuckle, anise, honey layers, green apple, balanced with crisp acidity and slight round viscosity

Recommendations
Tablas Creek Vineyard, "Espirit de Beaucastel Blanc" Paso Robles, California

Chateau du Trignon, Blanc du Blancs Rhône Valley, France

MING'S TIP

I'm a big advocate of rice cookers because they work. But for those who want to prepare rice traditionally, I always recommend the Mount Fuji method, detailed in the recipe. This involves adding enough water to the uncooked rice to reach the highest knuckle of a hand pressed against the rice. Follow this system, and your rice will always be fluffy.

MASTER RECIPE

TRY IT
Spiced Panko is the best possible breading for a wide range of cutlets, whether poultry, meat, or fish. Use it as part of a coating that also includes flour and eggs.

The panko makes a great topping for three-bean and other casseroles, or for vegetable gratins. Sprinkle it on top about 10 minutes before the dish is done.

For the best fried onion rings, soak onion slices in buttermilk for at least an hour and up to overnight. Coat with the panko and deep-fry at 375°F. until the rings are golden, 6 to 8 minutes.

SPICED PANKO BREAD CRUMBS

Can you fall in love with bread crumbs? I did when I first tried panko, the coarse Japanese bread crumbs that are also airier than Western kinds, and therefore make the most delicate crusts; they also fry to a gorgeous golden brown. I've long used panko for all my breading and found it superior even to homemade crumbs made with good bread.

Here, I've flavored panko with thyme, basil, ginger, and chile heat, which makes the crumbs a really exciting ingredient and one you'll use often. The flavored crumbs also store beautifully.

Makes 4 cups
Lasts 3 weeks, refrigerated

4 cups panko (Japanese bread crumbs)
2 tablespoons dried thyme
2 tablespoons dried basil
1 tablespoon powdered ginger
1 tablespoon coarsely ground black pepper
1 tablespoon ancho chile powder or regular chile powder

In a medium bowl, combine all the ingredients and mix well. Use or store.

BEVERAGE TIP
Grape type
Zinfandel

Characteristics
Explosion of ripe
blackberries, nutmeg,
licorice, rich mouthfeel
and long finish,
warm gentle spices

Recommendations
F. Teldeschi Winery
Dry Creek Valley,
California

Ravenswood
Sonoma County,
California

ASIAN MEATLOAF

I made my first meatloaf when I was fifteen, and it left a lot to be desired. I thought all you had to do to make meatloaf was put some ground meat in a pan and bake it. The result of this approach, when served, was a break-your-toe food-brick.

I've since earned my meatloaf credentials, and I offer this delicious East–West take on the classic as proof. Light, juicy, and spicy, too, it's superior in every way, thanks largely to the flavored panko in it. This comfort dish, served with a ketchup–sambal relish, is great hot, but you can also refrigerate it and serve it the next day. Or try it in sandwiches, an approach I love.

MING'S TIP
The meatloaf is made
from ground pork as
well as beef. The pork
adds flavor and
lusciousness to the
mixture. But you can
use ground beef
only, if you like.

Serves 4

¼ cup ketchup
¼ cup plus 1 tablespoon Traditional Spicy Sambal (page 56) or regular sambal
1½ pounds ground beef, chuck or round
1 pound ground pork
2 large onions, cut into ¼-inch dice
2 tablespoons minced garlic
2 tablespoons naturally brewed soy sauce
2 eggs, lightly beaten
¼ cup Worcestershire sauce
1 cup Spiced Panko Bread Crumbs (page 218)
Kosher salt and freshly ground black pepper to taste
3 bacon strips

1. Preheat the oven to 350°F. Oil a 1½-quart loaf pan and line the bottom with parchment paper. In a small bowl, combine the ketchup and the 1 tablespoon of sambal and set aside.

2. In a large nonreactive bowl, combine the ground beef and pork. Add the onions, garlic, the remaining ¼ cup of sambal, the soy sauce, eggs, Worcestershire sauce, and panko. Season with salt and pepper and, using your hand, mix well. Fill the pan with the mixture, top with the bacon, and bake until cooked through, about 45 minutes. Unmold, slice, and serve with the sambal mixture on the side as a condiment.

BEVERAGE TIP

Grape type

Riesling

Characteristics

Off dry, lychee, slight crisp peach melon, touch of viscosity, refreshing acids

Recommendations

Grosset Polish Hill Clare Valley, Australia

Dr. L, Riesling Mosel-Saar-Runer, Germany

MING'S TIP

When the crabs are out of season, try this dish using peeled and butter-flied jumbo shrimp. They'll take about 2 minutes to cook. Feel free to double the recipe for an entrée-size portion.

PANKO-CRUSTED SOFT-SHELL CRAB WITH DIM SUM DIPPER

Soft-shell crabs are strictly seasonal, one of the few foods that still are. The fact that you can't always have them makes them even more welcome when they do appear in early spring. You can grill them, but to my mind, pan-frying best delivers their spectacular taste and bursting juiciness. This panko-coated version offers those thrills plus an exceptionally crispy crust. Served with a dim sum dipping sauce, these are memorable.

Serves 4

1 cup all-purpose flour
3 eggs, lightly beaten
2 cups Spiced Panko Bread Crumbs (page 218)
Canola oil, for frying
4 medium soft-shell crabs, cleaned
Kosher salt and freshly ground black pepper to taste
2 large Belgian endive, cored and sliced 1/8 inch thick
Juice of 1 lemon
1/2 cup Dim Sum Dipper (page 76)

1. Place the flour, eggs, and panko crumbs in 3 separate shallow dishes.

2. Heat a large, heavy sauté pan over high heat. Add 1/2 inch of the oil and heat. Meanwhile, season the crabs with salt and pepper. Dredge them in the flour, shaking off the excess. Dip the crabs in the eggs and the panko, and fry, turning once, until golden brown, 2 to 3 minutes per side. Remove and drain on paper towels. Season with salt and pepper.

3. In a small bowl, combine the endive with the lemon juice. Season with salt and pepper and toss.

4. Place a small mound of the salad on each of 4 plates. Halve the crabs and place two halves on each salad portion. Serve with the Dim Sum Dipper.

222

BEVERAGE TIP

Grape type
Syrah or Syrah Blend
(with Carignan,
Mouvedre, Grenache,
and Cinsault)

Characteristics
New World South
Rhone styles, forward
expressive ripe fruits,
dash spice, cedar, wild
berries, licorice,
espresso, bitter
chocolate, wild herbs,
zesty lingering finish

Recommendations
Jaffurs Syrah
Santa Barbara County,
California

Fife Vineyards,
"L'Attitude 39"
Mendocino County,
California

MING'S TIP

Each breast needs to be
pounded to equal
thickness. Instead of
pounding, though, you
can slice from the center
of each breast to the
thickest side, stopping
just short of that side.
Fold the cut open as you
would open a book, and
you'll have a larger cutlet
of uniform thickness.

PANKO-CRUSTED CHICKEN SANDWICH

This is one of the most popular lunch dishes at Blue Ginger: a crispy, spicy chicken breast served in a sandwich with mustard, mayo, and shredded iceberg lettuce. I got the idea for it years ago from a college friend who—weirdly, I first thought—liked to wrap fried chicken pieces, bone and all, in squishy white bread before digging in. (He'd eat around the bone.) The bread would absorb the juices and provide additional chewy texture. I was soon converted to his tasty (and mess-free) innovation. This version is much, much suaver and even more addictive.

Serves 4

1 cup all-purpose flour
3 eggs, lightly beaten
2 cups Spiced Panko Bread Crumbs (page 218)
Canola oil, for frying
4 large skinless chicken breasts, pounded as needed for consistent thickness
Kosher salt and freshly ground black pepper to taste
2 tablespoons Dijon mustard
1/4 cup mayonnaise
4 sesame seed–topped buns, split
1 head of iceberg lettuce, shredded
1 large ripe tomato, cored and sliced 1/4 inch thick

1. Place the flour, eggs, and panko crumbs in 3 separate shallow dishes.

2. Heat a large, heavy sauté pan over high heat. Pour in 1/2 inch of oil and heat. Meanwhile, season the breasts with salt and pepper. Dredge them in the flour, shaking off the excess. Dip the breasts in the eggs and then the panko, and fry the breasts, turning once, until they are golden brown and their juices run clear when the breasts are pricked with the tip of a knife, 3 to 5 minutes per side. Remove and drain on paper towels.

3. Meanwhile, in a small bowl, combine the mustard and mayonnaise. To assemble the sandwiches, spread the mustard mixture lightly on the bun tops and bottoms. Top the bottoms with the lettuce, a fried breast, and tomatoes. Season the tomatoes with salt and pepper, and cover with the bun tops. Halve each sandwich and serve.

BROILED STUFFED EGGPLANT WITH BLACK PEPPER–GARLIC SAUCE

This great, all-vegetable dish owes its birth to Japanese as well as Chinese kitchen techniques. The Chinese often bake eggplant, which gives it deep flavor. The Japanese like to coat the vegetable with miso and then broil it. This dish, which works like twice-baked potatoes (baked and then mashed and restuffed), does both. A final napping with the Black Pepper–Garlic Sauce adds great flavor.

This makes a terrific starter and can be prepared ahead, up to the final broiling.

Serves 4

2 large eggplants
2 tablespoons extra-virgin olive oil
Kosher salt and freshly ground black pepper to taste
1 cup Spiced Panko Bread Crumbs (page 218)
$1/2$ cup scallions sliced $1/8$ inch thick
1 cup Black Pepper–Garlic Sauce (page 40)

1. Preheat the oven to 350°F.

2. Halve the eggplants lengthwise and, using a paring knife, score the flesh side about $1/2$ inch deep. Rub the flesh side with the olive oil and season with salt and pepper.

3. Transfer the eggplants flesh side down to a baking tray and bake until the flesh is soft enough to scoop from the skins, 30 to 45 minutes. Remove from the oven. Do not turn the oven off. Position a rack in the center of the oven.

4. Being careful to keep the skin intact, scoop the eggplant flesh into a large bowl. Add the panko, scallions, and $1/2$ cup of the Black Pepper–Garlic Sauce and toss well.

5. Mound the mixture into the eggplant shells and bake until hot, 8 to 10 minutes. Nap with the remaining sauce, transfer to the broiler, and broil until the surface is well colored, about 5 minutes. Serve immediately.

TRY IT

Use the rub to season scallops, then pan-fry them.

Season chicken thighs with the rub, then braise them in stock. Slow-cooking in liquid allows the tea to "steep," which brings out its subtle flavor.

For a deliciously different vegetable dish, trim and halve zucchini lengthwise, then coat all sides with the rub. Sear them in a medium-hot pan until cooked through and well colored, about 5 minutes.

MING'S TIP

This recipe calls for dried orange, lime, and lemon zests. You can sometimes buy these, but they're easy enough to make and have a lot of uses. Zest the fruit, spread the zests on a baking sheet, and bake at 200°F. until the zests are dried, about 2 hours. Store in a tightly sealed container in the fridge.

CITRUS HERBAL TEA RUB

I can never get enough of tea rubs, so I keep inventing new ones. This green tea and citrus example is particularly fresh and appealing: The tea is beautifully complemented by lemon, lime, and orange zest while mint and ginger add more invigorating flavor. This tea rub does wonders for lighter protein, like chicken and fish.

Makes about 4 cups
Lasts 3 weeks, refrigerated

1 cup green tea leaves
$1/2$ cup dried peppermint, spearmint, or mint
1 cup lemongrass powder or flakes
2 tablespoons sea salt or kosher salt
2 tablespoons turbinado sugar or raw sugar
$1/2$ cup dried orange zest (for this and the following zests, see Ming's Tip, left), crushed
$1/2$ cup dried lime zest
$1/4$ cup dried lemon zest
$1/4$ cup ground ginger

Combine all the ingredients in a small bowl. Use or store.

SEARED TEA-RUBBED CHICKEN BREASTS WITH CELERY SAUTÉ

I'm a celery freak. I love it raw with just a little salt, but I also sing its praises cooked, as a vegetable side. This dish features lemon-spiked sautéed celery, whose flavor really complements that of the rub-flavored chicken breasts. I remember once hearing that celery has minus calories because you expended more of them eating it than it contains. Putting aside that highly dubious observation, this dish is, nonetheless, very easy on the waistline.

Serves 4

1 cup Citrus Herbal Tea Rub (page 226)
4 boneless chicken breasts with skin
3 tablespoons grapeseed or canola oil
2 shallots, minced
1 head of celery, sliced diagonally ¼ inch thick (about 4 cups)
Juice and zest of 1 lemon
1 cup Master Chicken Broth (page 192) or low-sodium canned chicken stock
Kosher salt and freshly ground black pepper to taste
1 tablespoon unsalted butter

1. Spread the rub on a large plate and dredge the chicken breasts in it on both sides.

2. Heat a large sauté pan over medium heat, add 2 tablespoons of the oil, and swirl to coat the pan. Sauté the breasts, turning once, until cooked through, 4 to 5 minutes per side. Set the breasts aside and reheat the pan. Add the remaining tablespoon of oil, swirl to coat the pan, and add the shallots. Allow the shallots to sweat, about 1 minute. Add the celery and sauté, stirring, until just heated through, about 2 minutes. Add the lemon juice and zest and the broth, and season with salt and pepper. Cook until reduced by one quarter, 6 to 8 minutes. Whisk in the butter.

3. Slice the breasts diagonally ¼ inch thick. Divide the celery among 4 plates and arrange the chicken around it. Spoon the pan sauce over the chicken and serve.

CITRUS TEA–RUBBED HALIBUT WITH ORANGE–FENNEL ORZO SALAD

Delicate Citrus Herbal Tea Rub and mild sautéed halibut were made for each other. Here, the fish is served with a refreshing salad of raw fennel, orzo, and orange segments. This fast, all-in-one dish is especially welcome in summer.

Serves 4

$1/2$ cup Citrus Herbal Tea Rub (page 226)
Four 6-ounce halibut fillets
2 tablespoons grapeseed or canola oil
2 cups cooked orzo (from $1^1/2$ cups raw)
3 oranges, 2 segmented, 1 juiced
Juice of 1 lemon
2 medium fennel bulbs, stalks removed, halved vertically, cored, and sliced
$1/8$ inch thick
1 tablespoon extra-virgin olive oil, plus more for garnish
Kosher salt and freshly ground black pepper to taste

1. Spread the rub on a large plate and press the halibut into it on both sides.

2. Heat a large sauté pan over medium heat. Add the oil and swirl to coat the pan. Add the halibut and sauté, turning once, until the halibut is cooked through, 4 to 5 minutes per side.

3. Meanwhile, in a medium bowl combine the orzo, orange segments and juice, lemon juice, fennel, and olive oil and toss to coat. Season with salt and pepper.

4. Divide the salad among 4 serving plates, top with the halibut, drizzle some olive oil over, and serve.

TEA-RUBBED SHRIMP FRIED RICE

Fried rice is the first dish I ever cooked, at age ten, for hungry friends. The result was a little greasy, but no one seemed to care, and I was really proud of my effort. The dish is still one of my favorites, one I'm always trying to reinvent. This shrimp version is full of great flavor from the tea-rub in it, and is ready in minutes.

Serves 4

1 pound medium shrimp, peeled, deveined, and roughly chopped
$1/2$ cup Citrus Herbal Tea Rub (page 226)
4 tablespoons grapeseed or canola oil
3 eggs, lightly beaten
1 tablespoon minced garlic
1 tablespoon peeled and minced fresh ginger
6 cups cooked jasmine rice, cold (page 217)
1 cup frozen peas
1 tablespoon naturally brewed soy sauce
Kosher salt and freshly ground black pepper to taste

1. In a medium bowl, combine the shrimp and the rub and toss until the shrimp are evenly coated with the rub.

2. Heat a wok over high heat. Add 2 tablespoons of the oil and swirl to coat the pan. Add the eggs and scramble until almost cooked through, about 1 minute. Transfer the eggs to a plate.

3. Reheat the wok, add 1 tablespoon of the remaining oil to it, and swirl to coat the pan. Add the shrimp and stir-fry until almost cooked through, 2 to 3 minutes. Transfer to the plate with the eggs.

4. Reheat the wok, add the remaining tablespoon of oil, and swirl to coat the pan. Add the garlic and ginger and sauté, stirring, until fragrant, about 30 seconds. Add the rice and peas and toss. Return the eggs and shrimp to the wok and toss until all the ingredients are heated through, about 3 minutes. Add the soy sauce, season with salt and pepper, and serve immediately in rice bowls.

BEVERAGE TIP
Grape Type
Chardonnay

Recommendations
Maureau Naudet
Chablis
Burgundy, France

MING'S TIPS
If you want more
intensely flavored
scallops, rub them
before steaming them
with additional Citrus
Herbal Tea Rub

CITRUS HERBAL TEA–STEAMED SCALLOPS

Besides being delicately delicious, this is the heart-healthy dish. It's just flavored steamed scallops combined with fresh greens and a tantalizing vinaigrette. It also makes a nice change of pace when you've had too many rich foods, and you want something that's light yet satisfying.

There are many steamers out there. I use the traditional Chinese bamboo one, lined with a lettuce leaf. The bamboo adds a little flavor to the dish, and the steamer is easy to use. That said, I've also had good luck with Western steamers, and recently with automatic ones, which generate even heat and don't warmup the kitchen, a good thing in summer.

Serves 4

1 cup Citrus Herbal Tea Rub (page 226)
12 large scallops
Kosher salt and freshly ground black pepper to taste
$1/4$ pound mâche or other mixed small greens, water cress or upland cress
$1/4$ cup Five-Herb Vinaigrette (page 122) or other homemade vinaigrette

1. Fill the bottom part of a large steamer with 1 quart of water. Bring to a boil over high heat and add the tea rub.

2. Meanwhile, season the scallops with the salt and pepper. Spray the perforated steamer section with nonstick cooking spray, fit it over the pot, and add the scallops. Steam the scallops, covered, until just cooked through, 5 to 7 minutes.

3. Meanwhile, in a large bowl combine the mâche and vinaigrette and toss to coat. Season with the salt and pepper. Add the scallops and toss very lightly, Divide the salad among 4 plates and serve.

IN THIS CHAPTER

BLUE GINGER CRACKER
DOUGH

BUTTER SHORTBREAD
COOKIE DOUGH

TAHITIAN CRÈME ANGLAISE

BITTERSWEET CHOCOLATE
GANACHE

TROPICAL FRUIT SALSA

DOUGHS AND DESSERTS

People don't usually think that doughs are storable. That's unfortunate, because they freeze beautifully and, once on hand, can be turned into savory and sweet specialties with little effort. To make the point, I've come up with two easily made master doughs that store easily and are incredibly versatile. The savory dough is the basis for East-West treats, including Blue Ginger's signature garlic, spice, and pepper crackers; the best scallion pancakes; and fabulous burgers you enclose in the dough before they're cooked to make unique, all-in-one sandwiches. You can also just run with the dough, using it to wrap a whole tenderloin for a beef Wellington–type dish—or simply fry dough strips for a quick crunchy hors d'oeuvre or snack.

When it comes to the cookies, everyone can be happy, because, with Butter Shortbread Cookie Dough on hand, you can make such a big selection. These range from Five-Spice Shortbread, to a killer double chocolate-ginger version to Caramel Macadamia Nut Crunch.

Crème anglaise, the classic creamy French dessert custard, and the more recently devised chocolate ganache, a simple mixture of chocolate and cream, are usually thought of as, respectively, a dessert sauce and cake topping. But flavor and freeze crème anglaise, and you get fabulous ice cream—and you can transform ganache into impossible-to-resist chocolate truffles, the easiest of all candies to make at home, or into warm soufflé cakes served with a cardamom cream and my Asian Banana Split. I also present Tropical Fruit Salsa; you'll love it used in Tropical Fruit Yogurt Parfait and a refreshing granita; it's also the basis of a seriously delicious drink, Frozen Tropical Fruit Martinis. Talk about versatile!

TRY IT

Use the dough to wrap miniature franks for superior pigs in a blanket.

The dough makes a great pizza crust. Roll it into a ¼- to ½-inch-thick circle and proceed as you normally do when preparing pizza.

For a great hors d'oeuvre, cut the dough into 2 by ¼-inch sticks, deep-fry them, and pass the sticks with your favorite tomato or pesto dip.

BLUE GINGER CRACKER DOUGH

At the restaurant, we get tons of requests for this recipe, which is the basis of our much-loved house crackers (see page 239). But this easily made, garlic- and spice-spiked dough also produces great scallion pancakes (see page 240) and other treats, depending on how the dough is rolled and what's added to it. It also keeps beautifully: Freeze it in quarter- or half-pound quantities in airtight plastic bags, defrost it at room temperature, and you can fix the kind of baked specialties that make a meal.

You can make the dough by hand if you like, but it's way easier to use a standard mixer with a dough hook.

Makes about 4 pounds of dough
Lasts about 1 week, tightly wrapped and refrigerated, 3 to 4 weeks frozen

1 tablespoon cumin seeds
1 tablespoon coriander seeds
1 tablespoon fennel seeds
1 teaspoon black peppercorns
½ ounce (2 packages) active dry yeast
6½ cups bread flour
1 cup extra-virgin olive oil
2 tablespoons minced garlic
2 tablespoons kosher salt

1. Using a mortar and pestle or a spice grinder, grind the cumin, coriander, fennel, and peppercorns and combine them in a medium bowl. Set aside.

2. In a 5-quart mixer bowl, or very large bowl if working by hand, combine in this order the yeast, 2½ cups cold water, the flour, oil, garlic, and salt. Using a dough hook, mix at low speed until the flour's gluten is fully developed and the dough is smooth and doesn't tear easily when stretched, about 15 minutes. Remove the dough from the machine and knead in the spices. If working by hand, combine the yeast, flour, oil, and salt and mound the mixture on a work surface. With your fingers, make a well in the mixture. Add 2½ cups cold water to the well and, working with a pastry scraper or large fork, gradually incorporate the flour into the water, as if you were making fresh pasta. Work the dough into a rough ball and then knead in the garlic and the spice mixture. Continue to knead until the dough becomes smooth, 10 to 12 minutes.

3. Cover the dough with plastic wrap. If using immediately, allow the dough to rise in a warm place until doubled in bulk, about 1 hour. Otherwise, refrigerate or freeze until ready to use.

THE BLUE GINGER CRACKER

This super-cracker is the first thing a Blue Ginger customer eats, and therefore something I've put a lot of thought into. Flavored with garlic and tantalizing spices including fennel and coriander seed, it's everything a savory cracker should be and more. It's great with a meal, but you can also top the crackers with curried shrimp salad, tapenade, smoked salmon, or flavored cream cheese, for example, and serve them as an hors d'oeuvre. I confess I like them best as is, but you can do as Julia Child did when she visited us at the restaurant: slather them with butter. They're not bad that way—not bad at all.

Makes about forty 3 by 4-inch crackers

1 cup extra-virgin olive oil, plus more for the pans
1 egg white, for brushing
1 recipe Blue Ginger Cracker Dough (page 236)
Kosher salt to taste
¼ cup toasted sesame seeds (see Ming's Tip, right)

1. Preheat the oven to 350°F. In a small bowl, whisk the 1 cup of olive oil and the egg white and set aside.

2. If using defrosted frozen dough, allow it to double at room temperature, about 1 hour. Flour a work surface generously. Place the dough on it and with your hands, flatten the dough into a 1-inch-thick rectangle. Fold the dough in half and flatten it again into a similar rectangle. Wrap the dough in a damp cloth and allow it to rest for 15 minutes.

3. Grease 2 large baking sheets, preferably rimmed, with olive oil and set aside. Quarter the dough rectangle, and roll each piece ¼ inch thick, keeping the rectangle shape. Transfer 1 rectangle carefully to each of the pans and, using your hands, stretch the rectangles to the sides of the pan, making them as thin as possible without tearing. Using a pizza cutter, trim the dough edges. (Keep the trimmings, which can be combined and used to make more crackers.)

4. Brush the dough with the oil–egg white wash. Sprinkle the dough with salt and sesame seeds. Using a pizza cutter, cut the dough into 5 by 5-inch rectangles (or any size you like). Bake the crackers until lightly golden, about 20 minutes. Remove the crackers with a spatula and cool on racks.

BEVERAGE TIP
Beer

Characteristics
Light, crisp, refreshing, simple grains, barley nuance

Recommendations
Foster's, Australia

Sapporo, Japan

MING'S TIPS
A wash of egg white *plus* olive oil helps the salt and sesame seeds stick to the crackers better. You can use this trick when making other flat breads with a "dry" topping.

To toast sesame seeds, choose a heavy sauté pan that will hold the seeds in a single layer. Heat the seeds over medium heat and toast until golden, stirring constantly, about 8 minutes.

BEVERAGE TIP

Grape type
Pinot Gris

Characteristics
Simple starter,
light, refreshing,
apple, pear, honey,
mineral component

Recommendations
Bodega Lurton
Mendoza, Argentina

SCALLION PANCAKES

Everyone loves scallion pancakes, and once you have Blue Ginger Cracker Dough on hand, they couldn't be simpler to make. Yeh-Yeh, my paternal grandfather, used to stuff his scallion pancakes with ground pork or beef. For the ultimate version, why not treat the pancakes like pita bread or tortillas and wrap them around a beef stir-fry? Or fill them with cold chicken salad? The combination of the hot bread and the cold salad is tremendous.

These are served with a sambal-spiked dipping sauce.

Makes 4 pancakes

DIPPING SAUCE
1 tablespoon Traditional Spicy Sambal (page 56) or store-bought sambal
$1/4$ cup rice wine vinegar
$1/4$ cup naturally brewed soy sauce

1 tablespoon Asian sesame oil
3 tablespoons extra-virgin olive oil
1 pound Blue Ginger Cracker Dough (page 236)
2 cups scallions, white and green parts, cut diagonally $1/16$ inch thick
Kosher salt and freshly ground black pepper to taste
1 tablespoon grapeseed or canola oil

1. To make the dipping sauce, combine the sambal, vinegar, and soy sauce in a small bowl and mix. Set aside.

2. In a small bowl combine the sesame and olive oils and set aside.

3. Flour a work surface and on it roll the dough into a rectangle $1/8$ inch thick. Brush the dough with the oil mixture, sprinkle with the scallions, and season with salt and pepper.

RECIPE CONTINUES

4. Starting with one long side nearest you, roll the dough jelly-roll fashion to make a tight log. Cut the log into 4 equal pieces.

5. Roll 1 piece with your palms to make a skinnier log about $1/2$ inch in diameter. Twist each end of the log in opposite directions 4 or 5 times (this will make additional pancake layers), then wrap the log around itself to make a coil, tucking the outside end beneath the coil. With a rolling pin, flatten the coil to $1/4$ inch thick. Repeat with the remaining dough to make 3 more pancakes.

6. Heat a large nonstick sauté pan over medium heat. Add the grapeseed oil and swirl to coat the pan. Depending on the pan's size, add 1 to 2 pancakes and cook until brown and crispy on both sides, turning once, 2 to 3 minutes per side. Cook the remaining pancakes. Slice each pancake into 4 wedges. Serve the pancakes with the dipping sauce.

VARIATION

For a savory pancake addition, mix 2 cups of finely chopped raw shrimp in a bowl with the scallions. Sprinkle the dough evenly with the mixture, and proceed with the recipe, frying the pancakes 3 to 4 minutes per side.

ASIAN HAMBURGER POCKETS

As a kid, I used to spend many a summer visiting my grandparents, Yeh-Yeh and
Nai-Nai, in Taiwan. There I discovered *shiar-bing,* large, round, pot sticker–like dim
sum. These "hamburgers," made with seasoned ground beef and pork enclosed in
savory Blue Ginger Cracker Dough, are a takeoff on that traditional treat. Because
the meat is cooked in the dough, these all-in-one sandwiches are easy to make.

I like to serve a side salad with these.

Serves 4

1 pound Blue Ginger Cracker Dough (page 236)
1 pound ground beef
1 pound ground pork
1 cup scallions, white and green parts, cut $1/16$ inch thick
1 tablespoon peeled and minced fresh ginger
2 tablespoons naturally brewed soy sauce
Kosher salt to taste
1 teaspoon coarsely ground black pepper
2 tablespoons grapeseed or canola oil

1. Divide the dough into 4 equal pieces and shape each into a rough ball. Flour a
work surface, and on it roll the dough into ¼-inch-thick rounds.

2. In a large bowl, combine the beef, pork, scallions, ginger, soy sauce, salt, and
pepper and mix lightly. Divide the mixture into 4 equal parts and roll each into a
ball. Place 1 ball in the center of each piece of dough, bring up the sides, and twist
into a spiral to seal. Slightly flatten the dough-enclosed "burgers."

3. Heat a large nonstick sauté pan over medium heat. Add the oil and swirl to coat
the pan. Add the burgers, sealed end down, and cook until golden, 4 to 5 minutes.
Turn and cook for another 4 or 5 minutes. Allow the burgers to rest for about
4 minutes. Halve and serve immediately.

BUTTER SHORTBREAD COOKIE DOUGH

I'm really enthusiastic about this dough. It produces shortbread and other cookies that are everything they should be: buttery, just sweet enough, crisp, yet melt-in-your-mouth tender, too.

Some, me included, like their butter cookies plain. Others like them with flavorful additions, like chocolate. To satisfy everyone, this chapter offers both. To make the various cookies, you prepare dough logs, cut the cookies from them, and then "season" the unbaked rounds with sugar or another mixture. You can freeze the dough flavored or unflavored, in logs or not—or some of each. The recipe makes enough dough that you can always have some on hand—a great thing for all cookie lovers.

Makes 4 logs 10 inches long by 1 1/4 inches in diameter
Lasts 2 weeks, frozen

1 1/2 cups (3 sticks) unsalted butter, at room temperature
1 1/3 cups sugar
2 teaspoons kosher salt
3 egg yolks
2 tablespoons vanilla extract
Interior scrapings of 1/2 split vanilla bean, preferably Tahitian
3 3/4 cups all-purpose flour

1. In the bowl of a mixer, combine the butter, sugar, and salt and cream on medium speed until blended, about 2 minutes. One by one, add the egg yolks, mixing until incorporated. Add the vanilla extract and the scrapings of the vanilla bean. Scrape down the bowl.

2. Turn the mixer off and add the flour. Turn the machine to low and mix until the flour is completely incorporated. Remove the dough from the bowl. Working on parchment or wax paper, form the dough into 4 logs 10 inches long and 1 1/4 inches in diameter, wrap, and chill.

CLASSIC SHORTBREAD

Here's my favorite cookie, no contest. It's just unadulterated, buttery shortbread with a crunchy-sweet sugar topping.

Makes 20 cookies

1 cup granulated, raw, or turbinado sugar
1 chilled log of Butter Shortbread Cookie Dough (page 244)

1. Preheat the oven to 325°F. Place the sugar in a small bowl.

2. Cut the log into twenty $1/2$-inch rounds. Dip one cut surface of each of the rounds into the sugar and arrange them 2 inches apart on all sides on a parchment-lined or nonstick cookie sheet or sheets.

3. Bake until golden brown, 15 to 20 minutes. Cool the cookies on a wire rack.

BEVERAGE TIP
Grape type
Sémillon

Characteristics
Rich balance of crisp orange, tangerine peel, peach, honey and aromatics

Recommendations
Yalumba,
Botrytis Sémillon
Eden Valley, Australia

Chalk Hill, Botrytised
Semillon
Napa Valley, California

FIVE-SPICE SHORTBREAD

After much experimentation, I found a way to give the savory "warm" five-spice taste to sweets by substituting powdered ginger for the peppercorns.

Makes 20 cookies

2 teaspoons ground ginger
2 teaspoons ground cinnamon
2 teaspoons ground cardamom
$1/2$ teaspoon ground cloves
$1/2$ teaspoon ground star anise (see Ming's Tip, right)
$1/4$ cup turbinado or other granulated sugar
1 chilled log of Butter Shortbread Cookie Dough (page 244)

1. Preheat the oven to 325°F. In a small bowl, combine the ginger, cinnamon, cardamom, cloves, star anise, and sugar.

2. Cut the chilled log into twenty $1/2$-inch rounds. Dip one cut surface of each round into the spice mixture and arrange the rounds 2 inches apart on all sides on a parchment-lined or nonstick cookie sheet or sheets.

3. Bake until golden brown, 15 to 20 minutes. Remove the cookies with a spatula and cool on a wire rack.

BEVERAGE TIP
Ginger Tea
(sweetened with ginger simple syrup see *Blue Ginger*)

MING'S TIP
Grind star anise to a powder in a clean coffee grinder reserved for this purpose.

BEVERAGE TIP

Grape type

Tinta Roriz
(Tempranillo),
Tinta Barroca,
Tinta Cão

Characteristics

Rich graceful balance
of caramel, cocoa, and
sweet stewed plum and
cooked sour cherry

Recommendations

Ferreira,
Personal Reserve
"Doña Antonia"
Oporto, Portugal

Warrés, L.B.V.
(Late Bottled Vintage)
Oporto, Portugal

MING'S TIP

Extra-Brut cocoa, a
specialty cocoa available
at gourmet shops and
baking supplies stores,
makes extra-dark,
extra-rich cakes, cookies
and more. If you can't
find it, use any Dutch
process cocoa.

DOUBLE CHOCOLATE–GINGER SHORTBREAD

My personal discovery that chocolate and ginger make an awesome flavor combination occurred when I accidentally dropped some candied ginger in a bowl of ganache. I felt like the kid in the commercial for Reese's peanut butter cups when he realizes that peanut butter and chocolate are *it*. These addictive cookies benefit from the chocolate–ginger affinity, to say the least.

Makes 20 cookies

1/4 cup turbinado or other granulated sugar
1/4 cup extra-brut cocoa (see Ming's tip, left) or regular unsweetened cocoa
1 tablespoon peeled and grated fresh ginger
1/4 cup minced candied ginger
3/4 cup semisweet chocolate chips, or bittersweet chocolate chopped into small chunks
1 chilled log of Butter Shortbread Cookie Dough (page 244)

1. Preheat the oven to 325°F. On a large plate, combine the sugar, cocoa, gingers, and chocolate and mix. Set aside.

2. Cut the log into twenty 1/2-inch rounds. Firmly press one cut surface of each round into the cocoa mixture and arrange the rounds 2 inches apart on all sides on a parchment-lined or nonstick cookie sheet or sheets.

3. Bake until golden brown, 15 to 20 minutes. Remove the cookies with a spatula and cool on a rack.

BEVERAGE TIP

Recommendations

Kona coffee,
Hawaii

Jamaican Blue
Mountain coffee,
Jamaica

CARAMEL MACADAMIA NUT CRUNCH

These fabulous cookies contain a rich brittle made with macadamias.

Makes 20 cookies

1 cup sugar
1 cup heavy cream
1 pound macadamia pieces, or whole nuts, roughly chopped
1 chilled log of Butter Shortbread Cookie Dough (page 244)

1. Preheat the oven to 325°F. Grease a baking sheet, preferably rimmed.

2. In a medium saucepan, combine the sugar and $1/2$ cup of water. Heat over medium heat until the mixture begins to simmer, about 3 minutes. Cover the pan and continue to simmer, allowing steam from the cooking mixture to wash down the sides of the pan. Remove the cover and continue to simmer until the mixture turns golden, 7 to 8 minutes. Immediately remove from the stove, and, to avoid letting the mixture bubbling over, carefully pour the cream in a slow, steady stream into the pan; do not stir. Return the pot to the stove, reduce the heat to low, and, using a wooden spoon, gently stir the mixture until the cream is completely incorporated.

3. Transfer the caramel to a medium bowl, add the nuts, and stir to coat the nuts evenly. Transfer the mixture to a the baking sheet, spreading it evenly, and bake until dark brown, 12 to 15 minutes. Cool the brittle to room temperature and chop it mixture coarsely using a food processor, or a cleaver, or by hand.

4. Cut the log of dough into 20 $1/2$-inch rounds, press one cut side of each round into the brittle, and arrange the rounds 2 inches apart on all sides on a parchment-lined or nonstick cookie sheet or sheets.

5. Bake until golden brown, 15 to 20 minutes. Remove the cookies with a spatula and cool on a wire rack.

MASTER RECIPE

TRY IT
This is the perfect dessert sauce. Pour it over fresh berries, chocolate cake, bread puddings, and the like.

For an instant sabayon-type dessert, fold the crème anglaise into whipped cream.

MING'S TIPS
You'll have leftover egg whites when you make the sauce. Refrigerate and use them within 2 days, or freeze and defrost to use in soufflés, meringues, or low-cholesterol, whites-only omelets.

Though Tahitian vanilla beans, the darkest of all varieties, are the beans of choice for this recipe, you can use other kinds, such as Madagascan, with very good results.

Tahitian vanilla beans are relatively expensive, but can be stored in an airtight container and refrigerated. (I recommend storing the beans in sugar; this helps to preserve them, and you have a bonus of fragrant vanilla sugar for baking.)

TAHITIAN CRÈME ANGLAISE

Crème anglaise, a rich custard sauce that can be served hot or cold, is one of the world's great culinary creations. My version is even better, if I say so myself, because it's flavored with Tahitian vanilla beans, noted for their intense vanilla flavor, as well as with heavy cream. This isn't a diet specialty, of course, but one that's welcome as an occasional treat. It's also the basis for a number of super desserts, including a particularly fabulous vanilla ice cream.

Makes 6 cups
Lasts 1 week, refrigerated

2 vanilla beans, preferably Tahitian
1 quart heavy (whipping) cream
1 quart milk
2 cups sugar
16 extra-large egg yolks

1. With a paring knife, split the vanilla beans. Using a teaspoon, scrape their insides into a medium saucepan, and add the pods. In the same pan combine the cream, milk, and 1 cup of the sugar and cook over low heat, stirring, just until the mixture becomes hot, 10 to 15 minutes. Turn off the heat but leave the saucepan on the stove.

2. In a medium bowl, combine the yolks and the remaining cup of sugar and whisk until the sugar is dissolved and the mixture is pale yellow. Remove 2 cups of the cream mixture from the saucepan and, whisking constantly, add it gradually to the yolk mixture. Stir the lightened yolk mixture back into the saucepan and cook the custard over low heat, stirring constantly with a wooden spoon, until the sauce thickens sufficiently to coat the spoon, 5 to 8 minutes.

3. Srain the sauce and transfer it to a shallow pan. To avoid a skin forming on the cream, cover it with plastic wrap so the wrap touches its surface. Keep the edges of the wrap raised so steam can escape. Cool in the refrigerator for 4 hours or overnight. Use or store.

BEVERAGE TIP
Recommendations
Snifter of Meyers
Dark Rum

TAHITIAN VANILLA ICE CREAM

This is hands down the tastiest, creamiest, richest, most wonderful vanilla ice cream ever. Because it's made with a crème anglaise base, it has that irresistibly "chewy" texture, the mark of the best French ice creams. And because it's flavored with Tahitian vanilla bean, it's deeply aromatic. Once you have the crème anglaise on hand, it's also a snap to make, so much so that you'll want to try all the variations that follow.

Makes 6 cups

4 cups Tahitian Crème Anglaise (page 250)

Following the manufacturer's instructions, freeze the Tahitian Crème Anglaise in an ice-cream maker. Continue freezing the ice cream in the freezer, preferably overnight or at least 4 hours, and serve.

VARIATIONS

Chocolate Chip Ice Cream After freezing the ice cream in the ice-cream maker, fold in 2 cups of bittersweet chocolate chips.

Chocolate Chip Swirl Ice Cream After freezing the ice cream in the ice-cream maker, fold in 2 cups of bittersweet chocolate chips, then drizzle and fold in 1 cup softened Bittersweet Chocolate Ganache (page 256).

Coffee Ice Cream Reserve ¼ cup of the Tahitian Crème Anglaise and make the ice cream with the rest. Mix 3 tablespoons of instant coffee with the reserved cream. After freezing the ice cream in the ice-cream maker, fold in the coffee-flavored mixture.

Caramel Macadamia Nut Ice Cream Prepare the macadamia brittle on page 249. After freezing the ice cream in the ice-cream maker, fold in the nut mixture.

BEVERAGE TIP
Grape type
Chenin Blanc/Mathilde
Framboise

Characteristics
Crisp off dry tart berry
component with
refreshing acids

Recommendations
Kir Royale with Chateau
Moncontour
Loire, France

MING'S TIP
You'll need round,
shallow ovenproof
dishes about 4 inches
in diameter for this.
Small ceramic tart pans
are ideal, or make the
dessert in a single
larger dish 10 to
12 inches across.

BERRIES GRATINÉ

Here's another incredible dessert that's easy to make once you have Tahitian
Crème Anglaise in the fridge. All you do is fold fresh berries into a mixture of
Tahitian Crème Anglaise and whipped cream, which is then dusted with sugar and
broiled to make a crackling caramel topping. Everyone loves the granité's texture
and flavor contrasts.

Serves 4

1 cup heavy (whipping) cream
1 cup Tahitian Crème Anglaise (page 250)
1 pint raspberries
1 pint blackberries
Confectioners' sugar, for dusting

1. Preheat the broiler, or set the oven to 375°F. Butter four shallow ovenproof
baking dishes about 4 inches in diameter each (see Ming's Tip, right). Place on a
baking sheet.

2. In a chilled medium bowl, and using a chilled whisk, beat the cream until stiff.
Add the crème anglaise to the cream and, using a spatula, fold the two together.
Fold in the berries, fill the dishes with the mixture, and sprinkle heavily but evenly
with the confectioners' sugar.

3. Watching very carefully, broil the gratiné as far as possible from the heat source
until the tops are brown and bubbly, 4 to 6 minutes. Serve hot or cold.

BEVERAGE TIP
Grape type
Moscato (Bianco)

Characteristics
Intense, aromatic,
pale straw color,
nectar, orange apricot,
crisp herbal, musk,
citrus nuances

Recommendations
Nivole, Moscato d'Asti
Piedmont, Italy

MING'S TIP
If you don't find
unsweetened shredded
coconut in your super-
market, look in a natu-
ral or health food store
for dessicated coconut.

PINEAPPLE CUSTARD

I wish everyone loved pineapple as much as I do. This simple pudding should help the cause. Made with shredded coconut and flavored with rum, it's rich but also refreshing and definitely the thing to end a meal, whether simple or dressy.

For a special treat, serve this with additional Tahitian Crème Anglaise.

Serves 8

1/2 cup plus 2 tablespoons unsweetened shredded coconut
1 tablespoon unsalted butter
3 cups fresh pineapple cut into 1/4-inch dice, plus 1/2 cup diced pineapple
  for garnish
1/4 cup dark rum, preferably Barbados
3 cups Tahitian Crème Anglaise (page 250), plus additional for serving (optional)

1. Preheat the oven to 350°F. Butter eight 4-ounce ramekins and place them in a deep baking sheet or roasting pan.

2. In a medium nonstick sauté pan, toast the coconut over low heat, stirring constantly, until golden, 8 to 10 minutes. Set aside.

3. In a medium sauté pan, melt the butter over high heat. Add the 3 cups of pineapple and sauté until soft, stirring frequently, 2 to 3 minutes. Averting your face, add the rum and cook until the alcohol has evaporated completely, about 30 seconds. Transfer the pineapple to a large plate and allow to cool.

4. Pour the 3 cups of crème anglaise into a large bowl. Add 1/2 cup of the toasted coconut and all the sautéed pineapple and fold in. Divide the mixture among the ramekins. Pour enough hot water into the pan for it to come halfway up the sides of the ramekins and transfer them carefully to the oven. Bake until a knife inserted into the pudding comes out clean, 20 to 25 minutes. Cool to room temperature and refrigerate overnight. Garnish with the remaining 2 tablespoons of coconut and the diced pineapple, and serve with additional crème anglaise, if you like.

BITTERSWEET CHOCOLATE GANACHE

Ganache and I have a history. I almost OD'd on that simple but wonderful chocolate topping years ago at Fauchon in Paris, where I was challenged by Pierre Hermé, the esteemed pastry chef there, to scale up a ganache recipe. Involved were about two thousand dollars' worth of deluxe chocolate, cream, and a thirty-gallon kettle. I miscalculated the amount of cream needed for the new recipe and soon the kettle held ganache to the very, very rim. Pierre was not amused, and neither was I. It wasn't long before there was ganache everywhere, even inside my socks.

But only pleasure awaits you when you make this luscious dessert basic that's used in so many ways—as a frosting and glaze, for fillings, as a mousse and chocolate truffle base, and more. If you like to make sweets and you have ganache on hand, you're really way ahead.

Makes 5 cups
Lasts 2 weeks, refrigerated

3 cups heavy (whipping) cream, preferably not ultrapasteurized
2 tablespoons sugar
2 tablespoons (¼ stick) unsalted butter, cut into large dice
1 pound extra-bittersweet chocolate, roughly chopped

1. In a medium saucepan, combine the cream and sugar and heat over medium heat just until hot.

2. In a medium bowl, combine the butter and chocolate. Add the cream mixture and whisk until smooth. Pour the ganache into a shallow plastic or nonreactive metal container, and allow the ganache to cool to room temperature. Use or store, refrigerated.

WARM CHOCOLATE SOUFFLÉ CAKES WITH CARDAMOM CREAM

This dessert was the reason I hired our brilliant pastry chef, Marina Brancely. She auditioned with it, I tasted it, and she had the job. Light and moist, the individual cakes feature the dynamite combination of chocolate and cardamom. Their airy richness and deep chocolate flavor are perfectly complemented by the very fragrant spiciness of the cardamom cream. You must try this one.

Makes twelve 4-ounce cakes

4 cups Bittersweet Chocolate Ganache (page 256)
6 extra-large eggs
1/3 cup sugar

CARDAMOM CREAM
1 cup heavy (whipping) cream
1 tablespoon sugar
1 teaspoon powdered cardamom

1. Preheat the oven to 300°F. Grease twelve 4-ounce ramekins and line the bottoms with parchment or wax paper.

2. If the ganache has been chilled, warm it in a microwave oven at medium for 1 minute until it is completely melted and can be stirred easily. Or melt it in a metal bowl or saucepan submerged in a larger bowl or pan of hot water. If necessary, transfer the warmed ganache to a medium bowl and set aside.

3. Using a mixer set at medium speed, whip together the eggs and sugar until the mixture has tripled in volume, about 5 minutes for a standing mixer, 15 to 20 minutes for hand-held. Add the egg mixture to the ganache and fold the two together until thoroughly combined. Fill the ramekins three-quarters full with the batter. Place the ramekins in a deep pan or roasting pan and fill it with enough hot water to come halfway up the sides of the ramekins. Bake until the cakes are set but still moist, or until a paring knife inserted in them comes out with a coating that's still a bit gooey, 15 to 20 minutes. (If in doubt, underbake.)

4. Meanwhile, make the cardamom cream. Using a mixer, or by hand, whip the cream until lightly thickened. Add the tablespoon of sugar and the cardamom and continue whipping until stiff peaks form. Refrigerate until ready to use.

5. Top the cakes with the cardamom cream and serve warm.

BEVERAGE TIP
Grape type
Grenache

Characteristics
Cocoa, plum, fig, delicate refined velvety sweetness, light acid

Recommendations
Les Clos de Paulilles, Banyuls Languedoc-Roussillon, France

Serve chilled

BEVERAGE TIP

Grape type

Muscat

Characteristics

Tawny, sweetened
raisins, and plum and
cocoa, modest acids

Recommendations

Chambers,
Rosewood Muscat
Victoria, Australia

SESAME, MACADAMIA NUT, AND DRIED FRUIT CHOCOLATE TRUFFLES

Chocolate truffles are the most easily made homemade candy. All you need is some ganache and they almost make themselves. You can also flavor the basic truffles any way you like. This recipe features macadamias and dried fruit, but for more thrills, try adding candied ginger, walnuts or pine nuts, or even peanut butter. These are best eaten soon after making them, but you can also store them for 2 weeks in the fridge. You can halve this recipe, too.

Makes about eight dozen $1/2$-inch truffles

$1/2$ cup unsweetened cocoa powder
$1/2$ cup toasted sesame seeds (see Ming's Tip, page 239)
1 cup toasted and coarsely chopped macadamia nuts
1 cup coarsely chopped dried fruit, such as cranberries, cherries, golden raisins, pineapple, or mango
3 cups Bittersweet Chocolate Ganache (page 256)
Confectioners' sugar, for dusting (optional)

1. On separate plates, spread the cocoa powder, sesame seeds, macadamia nuts, and dried fruit (the types of fruit can be mixed or plated separately).

2. Using a mixer with the paddle attachment, whip the ganache at high speed until thickened and pale in color, about 30 seconds. With a 1-ounce ice-cream scoop or teaspoon, scoop portions of the ganache to make truffles about $1/2$ inch in diameter. Roll each truffle in the cocoa powder, sesame seeds, macadamia nuts, or chopped fruit, and dust some or all with the confectioners' sugar, if you like. If serving the truffles the same day, keep them in a cool place (not refrigerated) until served. If serving them later, refrigerate them, then allow them to come to room temperature before serving them. (You may have to re-roll the refrigerated truffles in cocoa and/or confectioners' sugar, if using.)

BEVERAGE TIP
Grape type
Tinta Roriz
(Tempranillo),
Tinta Barroca,
Tinta Cão

Characteristics
Caramel nut, orange
peel, cooked raisins

Recommendations
Dow's 20 Year Tawny
Oporto, Portugal

BITTERSWEET CHOCOLATE POTS DE CRÈME

This luxurious, deeply chocolaty dessert is a cinch to make once you have Bittersweet Chocolate Ganache and Tahitian Crème Anglaise on hand. You can knock out 20 or more of these in a flash, and your guests will applaud your "hard work."

Serves 8

1 cup Bittersweet Chocolate Ganache (page 256)
2 cups Tahitian Crème Anglaise (page 250)

1. Preheat the oven to 300°F. If the ganache has been chilled, warm it in a microwave oven on medium for 1 minute, until it can be stirred easily. Or put it in a metal bowl or saucepan submerged in a larger bowl or pan of hot water.

2. Add the crème anglaise to the ganache and stir to blend well. Place eight 3-ounce ramekins in a deep pan or roasting pan and fill the ramekins equally with the ganache mixture. Fill the deep pan with enough hot water to come halfway up the sides of the ramekins and bake until the pots de crème are just set (they should jiggle when the ramekins are gently shaken), 45 to 50 minutes. Chill well before serving.

ASIAN BANANA SPLIT

People sometimes laugh when I say there's no more perfect dish than a banana split. But well made, it balances different tastes, textures, and temperatures to the deep satisfaction of all who enjoy it. This version, made with ganache, toasted macadamias, rum, and Tahitian Vanilla Ice Cream, is more refined than the usual soda-fountain kind, but don't hold that against it! If you have the ganache and the ice cream on hand, it's not a big deal to make.

Serves 4

1 cup Bittersweet Chocolate Ganache (page 256)
1 tablespoon unsalted butter
4 bananas, each split lengthwise into thirds (12 pieces total) and cut into
    1/2-inch dice
1/4 cup dark rum, such as Barbados or Myers's
Juice of 1 lime
1/4 cup coarsely chopped toasted macadamia nuts
1 quart Tahitian Vanilla Ice Cream (page 252), or premium store-bought
    ice cream
Whipped cream, for garnish

1. If the ganache has been chilled, warm it in a microwave oven at medium for 1 minute, until it can be stirred easily. Or put it in a metal bowl or saucepan submerged in a larger bowl or pan of hot water.

2. In a large nonstick sauté pan, melt the butter over medium-high heat. Add the bananas and sauté, stirring, until they caramelize, about 1 minute. Avert your face from the pan, add the rum, and ignite the rum with a long match or by exposing it to a burner flame. When the alcohol has burned away, 15 to 30 seconds, cook until the liquid is reduced by half, 2 to 3 minutes. Add the lime juice and macadamia nuts and sauté, stirring, until heated through, about 1 minute.

3. Divide the ice cream among 4 serving bowls. Top with the banana mixture and the ganache. Garnish with the whipped cream and serve.

BEVERAGE TIP
Grape type
Riesling

Characteristics
Peaches, apricots, and slight spice

Recommendations
Mt. Horrocks, Cordon Cut Riesling Clare Valley, Australia

MING'S TIP
The recipe requires bananas that are split into thirds. To do this easily, run a fingertip along the length of each peeled banana, which will split into thirds "automatically."

MASTER RECIPE

TRY IT
This makes a delicious
topping for pancakes or
waffles, or vanilla ice
cream. Or try it as an
accompaniment to white
or pound cake. It's
particulary good with
coconut cake.

The salsa can be con-
verted to a savory version:
Add sliced scallions or
diced red onion plus a
pinch of salt to the salsa,
and serve it as a topping
for grilled fish.

MING'S TIP
Sharlyn melon tastes
deliciously like a cross
between honeydew and
cantaloupe. Ripe melons
have pretty orange-white
flesh; use them quickly, as
they soften rapidly after
ripening. If unavailable,
substitute a fifty-fifty
mixture of honeydew and
cantaloupe.

TROPICAL FRUIT SALSA

Salsa isn't just for tortilla chips. A sweetened version, made with fruits like mango and papaya, is wonderful as a dessert topping. (I call this a salsa because the fruit used is diced rather than puréed, which would make the topping a sauce.) Use all of the fruit called for in the recipe, or play with the quantities or kinds to suit you. In any case, you'll have a great, really versatile dessert accompaniment.

Makes 7 cups
Lasts 1 week, refrigerated

1 cup mango cut into ¼-inch dice
1 cup small papaya (strawberry papaya) or regular papaya cut into ¼-inch dice
1 cup sharlyn or other melon cut into ¼-inch dice (see Ming's Tip, left)
2 cups pineapple cut into ¼-inch dice
¼ cup pure passion fruit juice (available in specialty markets), or seeded and
   puréed fresh passion fruit flesh
¼ cup minced fresh mint
10 kaffir lime leaves, or the zest of 3 limes, minced
1 tablespoon peeled and minced fresh ginger
¼ cup Amaretto liqueur
½ cup fresh orange juice
¼ cup fresh lime juice
2 tablespoons sugar

1. In a large bowl, combine the mango, papaya, melon, pineapple, passion fruit juice, mint, and kaffir lime leaves. Set aside.

2. In a medium nonreactive saucepan, combine the ginger, Amaretto, orange juice, lime juice, and sugar. Bring to a simmer over medium heat, decrease the heat to low, and simmer the mixture until it is reduced to a light glaze, or by about one quarter, 10 to 15 minutes. Allow the glaze to cool slightly, pour over the fruit, and mix. Use or store.

BEVERAGE TIP
Sake

Characteristics
Silky mouthfeel,
high acids, super
delicate off dry banana
and rose petal aromas

Recommendations
Kijoshu Seiryo, Japan

MING'S TIP
This is great as is, but
try sprinkling the
parfaits with granola
before serving them.
Or accompany them
with shortbread or
other butter cookies.

TROPICAL FRUIT YOGURT PARFAIT

As the movie character Shrek said, "Everyone likes parfaits." This delicious version definitely has in-a-pinch virtues, but it also tastes like a serious dessert. The yogurt adds tart balance to the salsa, and mint contributes a note of spicy freshness. All you need is parfait or other tall glasses for serving the dessert. (If you use partic-ularly tall glasses, add more than two layers of the salsa and yogurt.)

Serves 4

4 cups plain nonfat yogurt
4 cups Tropical Fruit Salsa (page 264)
4 sprigs of fresh mint

Fill 4 parfait or other tall glasses, or wineglasses, with half of the yogurt. Top each portion with ¾ cup of the salsa. Top with the remaining yogurt and salsa and garnish with the mint. Chill before serving.

TROPICAL FRUIT GRANITA

Here's a homemade sorbet-like dessert you can make without the usual frozen-dessert hassle. All you do is combine the salsa with sparkling wine and freeze the mixture overnight. Because alcohol freezes at a lower temperature than other liquids, the dessert remains somewhat soft and can be scraped into serving bowls. This "instant granita" also works beautifully as a mid-meal intermezzo as it's not too sweet—just refreshing.

Serves 4

4 cups Tropical Fruit Salsa (page 264)
2 cups Champagne, other sparkling wine, or carbonated water

1. In a food processor, purée the salsa, add the wine, and pulse a few times to blend.

2. Transfer the mixture to ice-cube trays minus the cube grid, or to a square or rectangular container at least 2 inches deep, and freeze overnight. Just before serving, scrape the mixture using the back of a large fork to make large flakes. Serve the granita in chilled bowls.

FROZEN TROPICAL FRUIT MARTINIS

Martini variations can be odd, but these are delicious.

For 1 drink

1 cup Tropical Fruit Granita (above), frozen in an ice cube tray
1 ounce Midori melon liqueur
$1/2$ ounce Coco López (cream of coconut)
1 tablespoon Tropical Fruit Salsa (page 264), for garnish (optional)

In a blender, blend together the Tropical Fruit, Midori liqueur, ice cubes, and Coco López. Pour into a frozen martini glass and garnish with the Tropical Fruit Salsa on top, if using.

INDEX